FAMILY
RESEARCH
METHODS

FAMILY STUDIES TEXT SERIES

Series Editor: RICHARD J. GELLES, *University of Rhode Island*
Series Associate Editor: ALEXA A. ALBERT, *University of Rhode Island*

This series of textbooks is designed to examine topics relevant to a broad view of family studies. The series is aimed primarily at undergraduate students of family sociology and family relations, among others. Individual volumes will be useful to students in psychology, home economics, counseling, human services, social work, and other related fields. Core texts in the series cover such subjects as theory and conceptual design, research methods, family history, cross-cultural perspectives, and life course analysis. Other texts will cover traditional topics, such as dating and mate selection, parenthood, divorce and remarriage, and family power. Topics that have been receiving more recent public attention will also be dealt with, including family violence, later life families, and fatherhood.

Because of their wide range and coverage, Family Studies Texts can be used singly or collectively to supplement a standard text or to replace one. These books will be of interest to both students and professionals in a variety of disciplines.

Volumes in this series:

1. LATER LIFE FAMILIES
   Timothy H. Brubaker

2. INTIMATE VIOLENCE IN FAMILIES
   Richard J. Gelles & Claire Pedrick Cornell

3. BECOMING A PARENT
   Ralph LaRossa

4. FAMILY RESEARCH METHODS
   Brent C. Miller

5. PATHS TO MARRIAGE
   Bernard I. Murstein

Volumes planned for this series:

THEORIES OF FAMILY LIFE, David M. Klein

WORK AND FAMILY LIFE, Patricia Voydanoff

FAMILY POWER, Maximiliane Szinovacz

FAMILY STRESS, Pauline Boss

DIVORCE, Sharon J. Price & Patrick C. McHenry

REMARRIAGE, Marilyn Ihinger-Tallman & Kay Pasley

CONCEPTUAL FRAMEWORKS FOR FAMILY STUDIES,
   Keith Farrington

FAMILY RESEARCH METHODS

Brent C. Miller

FAMILY STUDIES
TEXT SERIES 4

SAGE PUBLICATIONS
Beverly Hills   London   New Delhi

Dedicated to Reuben Hill (1912-1985)
Family Scholar, Mentor, and Friend

For information address:

SAGE Publications, Inc.
275 South Beverly Drive
Beverly Hills, California 90212

SAGE Publications India Pvt. Ltd.
M-32 Market
Greater Kailash I
New Delhi 110 048 India

SAGE Publications Ltd
28 Banner Street
London EC1Y 8QE
England

Printed in the United States of America

Library of Congress Cataloging-in-Publication Data

Miller, Brent C.
 Family research methods.
 (Family studies text series; v. 4)
 Includes index.
 1. Family—Research. 2. Family—Research—
Methodology. I. Title. II. Series.
HQ728.M488 1986   306.8'5'072   86-964
ISBN 0-8039-2143-8
ISBN 0-8039-2144-6 (pbk.)

FIRST PRINTING

Contents

Preface

RESEARCH METHODS TEXTS are "how to" books. They tell how studies should be conducted to answer research questions. There are many social or behavioral research methods books, but few of them feature marriage and family examples (Adams and Schvaneveldt, 1985, is an exception). The relatively few sources in family studies that emphasize research methodology tend to be written for professionals rather than students. There are, for example, several chapters in the classic *Handbook of Marriage and the Family* (Christensen, 1964) devoted to family measurement (Straus, 1964), prediction studies (Bowerman, 1964), field studies (Nye, 1964) and demographic analyses (Glick, 1964). Monographs about family measurement (Straus and Brown, 1978) and methods (Winter and Ferreira, 1969) have occasionally appeared. In 1982 the *Journal of Marriage and the Family* devoted an entire issue to family research methodology as did the *Journal of Family Issues* in 1984. Advanced methodology summary statements are continuing to be written for professionals (Larzelere and Klein, in press), but most methodological writing in family studies has appeared in hundreds of widely scattered journal articles.

Unlike this professional literature to which I have referred, the present text has been written as a simple "primer." It is an elementary research methods text that uses marriage and family examples. I have tried to write informally and to keep the text brief and basic so that both upper division undergraduates and beginning graduate students could understand and benefit from it.

I am indebted to many mentors and colleagues who have helped me learn about marriage and the family and how it can be studied. Jay Schvaneveldt was an excellent first methods teacher at Utah State, and when I was at Minnesota, Joan Aldous, David Olson, and Ira Reiss all helped me gain a better understanding of marriage and family research methods. David Klein and Steven Jorgensen, two of my graduate student buddies, have been especially helpful over the years in integrating my understanding of research methodology (Klein et al., 1978). Although he was not best known as a methodologist, Reuben Hill was probably more influential than anyone else in shaping my thinking about marriages and families as objects of scientific study. After leaving Minnesota I had the delightful learning experience of team teaching a graduate research methods course with Jo Lynn Cunningham at the University of Tennessee. More recently, I had the good fortune to collaborate with Boyd Rollins and Darwin Thomas in writing an overview about marriage and family research methods (Miller et al., 1982). To all of these friends and teachers I am greatly indebted for what they have helped me to learn.

I must also thank Richard Gelles and Alexa Albert, the series editor and associate editor, for pushing me to get this text onto paper and for not giving up when I had fallen behind. I likewise appreciate anonymous reviewers of the manuscript, especially the most critical reviewer from whom I benefited the most. I also thank Sally Carles for patiently revising the manuscript, and the editors at Sage who have continued to be interested in this book long after it was to have been completed.

Brent C. Miller
Logan, Utah
December 1985

CHAPTER

1

Introduction to Studying Families

Whatever else it may be, science is a way of generating and testing the truth of statements about events in the world of human experience.
                                                                    Walter E. Wallace

ALL OF US KNOW about marriages and families. Parents, siblings, spouses, children—these are not remote academic subjects but virtually everyone's first-hand experiences. In addition to direct experiences we learn much about marriage and family life through observations of those around us, from the mass media, and from literature and drama. Many of our views about marriage and family life are shaped by religious and political traditions. Religious doctrines and state laws have institutionalized expected marriage and family behavior in human societies everywhere. Doctrine and laws, for example, frequently regulate the choice of marriage partners by age and relatedness, confine sexual relations to marriage, limit the number of children permitted (as in contemporary China), and specify the rights and obligations of spouses. In sum, our own experiences, family traditions, religion, and law generally address the *normative* aspects of marriage and family life, the shoulds and oughts, what is expected, considered good and bad, right and wrong.

In addition to our personal experiences and everyday observations, and quite apart from legal and religious norms, however, marriages and families can be understood in yet another way. Sometimes we want to know the answers to "What is?" marriage and family questions. Such questions usually cannot be answered accurately by our personal insights or by referring to normative prescriptions about what is right and wrong. For example:

- What is the average age at first marriage?
- How are mate selection choices made?
- What proportion of marriages end in divorce?
- Are those who marry when they are young more likely to divorce than those who marry when they are older?
- How do home environments and parent-child relations affect children's development?
- How do children's presence and characteristics affect parents?
- How widespread is physical violence between family members?
- Is a prevention or intervention program effective in reducing problem behaviors in families?

Like the examples above, some questions about marriage and family relations can be addressed empirically; that is, information or data can be gathered and assessed in a systematic way to help us better understand what happens in marriages and families and why. An *empirical* approach to understanding marriages and families relies on collecting and analyzing data to answer questions like those posed above.

A normative approach deals with questions such as whether or not unmarried people should have sexual relations. *Normative* questions are addressed by law, religion, and tradition. Empirical questions, on the other hand, can be addressed through scientific research. Carefully collected empirical data can help us better understand marriages and families by providing a counterbalance to our personal observations and folk wisdom, and tempering our tendency to make unfounded or biased assertions about the world around us.

SCIENCE AND FAMILY RESEARCH

Science has become a well-established enterprise in most developed societies. The business of science is the creation or discovery of knowledge. Scientists seek information about and explanations of the natural and social world by conducting empirical research. Marriages and families are aspects of human societies that for many reasons need to be better understood, and so they have become the focus of scientific research.

Put very simply, some assumptions underlying science are as follows:

(1) There are natural phenomena "out there" in the real world that exist independently of human perceptions.
(2) There are patterns or regularities in these natural phenomena.
(3) These patterns in natural phenomena can be observed through the use of scientific procedures.

The term *research* has several meanings to the lay person. For example, someone might do research about the average age at first marriage by looking up figures in a census report. Or, as part of a college course, one might write a research paper about the relationship between age at marriage and divorce. In this case one would probably spend time in a library finding, reading, and summarizing studies already done on this topic. In both of these examples, the basic idea of research is searching for information in response to a specific question for which one does not have a ready answer.

However, scientific family research as discussed in this book is a considerably more complex endeavor than looking up an answer or doing a library search. In order to arrive at the average age of first marriages, for example, someone had to devise a plan, make the necessary arrangements, collect the data, separate first from subsequent marriages, do the statistical computations, and disseminate the results. Scientific research not only begins with a question, but it also includes the systematic acquisition, analysis, and interpretation of empirical data from which conclusions can be drawn. In short, *science* is a collective and disciplined search for knowledge engaged in by professional scientists; scientific *research* is the structured and systematic process of inquiry in which they are engaged.

Scientific research is sometimes further divided into basic and applied categories, although they are not totally distinct. *Applied* research is done so that the knowledge obtained can be utilized or applied by policymakers, sponsors, or practitioners. Applied marriage and family researchers might, for example, study the effectiveness of various approaches to marital therapy or treatment of parents who abuse their children. *Basic* or *pure* research, by contrast, is the pursuit of knowledge for its own sake. Sometimes politicians or taxpayers question the legitimacy of basic research (e.g., Proxmire's Golden Fleece Award), but it is often difficult to tell when research that appears to be esoteric will result in an important finding that can be applied. Scientists often conduct basic research simply to better understand marriages and families, or they might be looking for results that can be quickly applied. In all cases, family researchers seek to acquire knowledge about empirical patterns and regularities.

KINDS OF SCIENCE

Science can be subdivided into various areas of study. A distinction is often made between the physical sciences (physics, geology, etc.), the life sciences (botany, zoology, etc.), and the social-behavioral sciences (psychology, sociology, etc.). Marriage and family research is a branch of, or most closely related to, the social-behavioral sciences. All sciences share an empirical approach to data collection and analysis, although some strategies and methods might be different.

Hard Science

Older physical science disciplines, such as physics or chemistry, have been able to refine their research methods to become increasingly precise and exact. The younger social-behavioral sciences that study human behavior and relationships are sometimes considered to be less precise and exact. The terms *hard* and *soft* sciences have arisen to describe this situation. Perhaps this is because the subject matter of the physical sciences lends itself more readily to controlled observation and analysis. No one knows how much more exact and precise the social and behavioral sciences will become over time. Some think that human behavior and social relationships are fundamentally different (and intrinsically softer) than phenomena studied in the so-called hard sciences. Such views are sometimes described in rather cynical terms: "From the perspective of the physical and biological sciences, human social life is only a small irregular scab on the face of nature, not particularly amenable to deep systematic analysis" (Goffman, 1983: 17). However, many social and behavioral scientists—myself included—continue to be guided by the belief that human behavior and social relations can be profitably investigated and better understood through empirical research. And, in recent years, there have been increasing doubts about how absolute and deterministic even the so-called hard sciences are (Doherty, 1984).

Social-Behavioral Sciences

Family researchers, and social scientists in general, sometimes compare their tools and procedures—their methods of knowing—with those used in the physical or natural sciences. These comparisons often are aimed at supporting or refuting the essential similarity of their scientific procedures. Those who emphasize similarities note that both social scientists and natural scientists rely on empirical evidence, develop general theories, strive to minimize personal value biases, investigate regularities, and use statistical techniques. Others assert that it is impossible to observe or measure some social variables, that trying to measure social variables changes them, that too many factors are involved to make causal assertions, that replication is difficult or impossible given the dynamic nature of social phenomena, and that true experimental manipulation and control are impossible for most social phenomena (Wagenaar, 1981: 3). Regardless of these contemporary debates about differences and similarities, a useful and increasingly respected science of marriage and family life has gradually emerged.

Family Science

During the mid- to late 1800s, Fredrick LePlay and Emile Durkheim found families and family variables to be of interest in their pioneering studies of social life. LePlay (1855) studied whole families by observing them and asking questions, and for that reason he has been called the first social researcher and family researcher (LaRossa and Wolf, 1985). By studying public records, Durkheim (1951) found that married people were less likely to kill themselves than singles, a fact that became part of his "social integration versus anomie" explanation of suicide behavior. Both of these men were unusual for their time in that they systematically collected and analyzed data about family members and their relationships.

Empirical research focusing specifically on understanding marriages and families per se, however, did not seriously get under way until well into the twentieth century (Christensen, 1964; Howard, 1981). Those who first studied marriages and families were relatively disadvantaged, as were other scholars of their time, by a lack of scientific tools; and indeed, it is not surprising that most of their research strategies (observations, case studies, interviews, etc.) originated in, or have a great deal in common with, the general methods of social and behavioral research that were then being devised.

In sum, family research methods and empirical data about families have been seriously and consciously developed for only a little over 50 years. Many disciplines have contributed to the scientific study of families, most notably sociology, psychology, and anthropology. And, in fact, many marriage and family researchers are closely affiliated with these and other base disciplines. In recent years an academic unit called *family studies* or *family science* has emerged at many universities to focus the efforts of marriage and family researchers from diverse disciplinary backgrounds (Burr and Leigh, 1983).

GOALS OF SCIENCE

Regardless of how similar or different the scientific study of families is to the hard sciences or to the social and behavioral sciences, all scientific research seems to share similar goals and some basic principles. Although the goals of science can be debated, they often have been characterized as description, explanation, prediction, and control.

Description

Description is the most basic activity and goal of science. Family researchers seek to describe the averages or central tendencies of marriage and family phenomena such as the age of marriage and number of children. Marriage and parenting attitudes and behaviors are also objects of scientific description. How many? How much? How often? Describing marriages and families is a largely empirical process that often relies on counting, frequencies, percentages, and descriptive statistics including measures of central tendency and dispersion.

Explanation

Explanation provides a sense of understanding by attempting to provide reasons for *why* something happens or is the way it is. Scientists seek to explain marriage and family life by identifying antecedents and consequences of the behaviors of interest. For example, the antecedents of mate selection choices can be better understood through various explanations, including background similarities, personality attributes, compatible goals and role expectations, and cultural norms about who chooses and who should be chosen.

Prediction

Prediction is being able to tell in advance that something will happen. It has been argued that prediction relies on the same theoretical and empirical basis as explanation; that is, the same ideas and relationships must be understood in order to explain what has happened and why, or to forecast what is likely to occur. Knowing the extent of partner congruence in values, role expectations, and background characteristics, for example, might be modestly predictive of marital compatibility and stability.

Control

When natural phenomena are well enough understood so that they can be explained and predicted, it is sometimes possible to exert *control* over them. In the social and behavioral sciences control takes various forms such as prevention, intervention, or therapy. For example, a therapist or practitioner might be able to intervene and help family members reduce or eliminate (control) an undesirable marriage or family behavior. Family violence, especially child and spouse abuse, are coming to be better understood and those at greatest risk can be better identified. Controlling family violence includes various approaches such as providing support, reducing isolation and situational stresses, giving individual and family therapies, and providing shelters during times of greatest difficulty.

BASIC PRINCIPLES OF SCIENCE

Objectivity and replicability are fundamental scientific principles. Objectivity is a way of approaching a question or problem. It means that scientists set up their procedures, as far as possible, "outside themselves" (Kerlinger, 1979). In other words, *objectivity* means that conditions are arranged so that personal or subjective elements enter into the research as little as possible. Of course, scientists are not devoid of values and research is never fully objective; the problems studied, the questions asked, and especially how the data are interpreted reflect the values of researchers (Baumrind, 1980; Gergen, 1982). The ideal of scientific inquiry into marriage and family phenomena is to conduct research in such a way that the procedures and results become public and can be replicated. *Replication* means that the findings of a study can be reproduced by other researchers following the same or similar procedures.

An important distinction can be made here between scientists, who have biases and values, and scientific procedures, which are public conventions. If procedures are objective and public, other researchers can follow them and replicate—or perhaps refute—the findings (Popper, 1965). Of course, exact replications of marriage and family events and relationships are not possible, but if patterns are strong or consistent enough to be repeatedly discerned by many investigators studying different subjects, greater confidence can be placed in them. When the same empirical finding is produced in many different studies the result is sometimes called an *empirical generalization*.

"In other words, objectivity helps researchers 'get outside' themselves, helps them achieve publicly reproducible conditions, and hopefully to attain publicly ascertainable findings" (Kerlinger, 1979: 10). Objectivity makes replication possible, and converging findings from many investigations are more convincing than results from a single study.

THE ELEMENTS OF SCIENTIFIC THOUGHT

Concepts

One of the most fundamental elements in scientific thought is a *concept*. A concept is a mental abstraction of particular things or events, and it consists of both a word or label and its meaning or definition. For example, we use the term *marriage* to refer to a concept understood by most adults regardless of whether or not they themselves are married. Marriage is generally understood to be a socially and legally recognized heterosexual relationship established with the expectation of permanence. Depending on the cultural context, the concept of marriage might also include expectations about reproduction, patriarchy or equalitarianism, and so on.

It is critically important for researchers to be clear about the concept under study. Broad concepts like marriage usually need to be broken into more specific concepts for research purposes. Studies about "marriage," for example, might be more precisely about mate selection, marital satisfaction, marital adjustment, marital stability, marital conflict, marital power, marital communication, marital violence, and so on. Similarly, the study of "sex" in family research might have to do with differences and similarities between males and females (biological sex), with sexual relationships such as intercourse, with societal sex-role stereotypes of what men and women are expected to do, with actual gender role behaviors of marital partners, or with the development of gender identity in children. Conceptual clarification and precision is a critically important beginning point in marriage and family research.

Variables

A variable is simply a concept that varies; that is, it assumes or can have two or more values. The concept of marital status is a variable that has two or more values. We could choose to use this variable with only two values (married and not married), but it usually makes more sense to include all of the logically possible values of the variable in our research (single, never married; currently married; legally separated or divorced; widowed, deserted, remarried, etc.).

It is particularly important to understand how variables vary. The simplest form of variation is *presence or absence*. Pregnancy is an example of an either/or variable; the female being studied might be either pregnant or not pregnant.

Another important way that variables vary is called *categorical*. Biological sex (gender) is probably the most widely used categorical variable in the study of human beings and their relationships; it has two relatively distinct categories, male and female. Marital status is another example of a categorical variable, but one that has more than two categories.

A third kind of variation in variables is called *continuous*; some variables vary along a continuous range. In other words, they vary in amount rather than kind. The concept of pregnancy might be measured as a variable in a sample of females by noting its presence or absence; however, the length of pregnancy among those who are pregnant might be an important continuous variable. The length of pregnancy is a continuous variable that can range from a few hours, days, or weeks, to nine months or more. There are many kinds of continuous variables besides those having to do with age or time. Frequencies reflect continuous variables (the frequency of smiling, touching, talking, spanking, and so on). The quality of many behaviors also reflects continuous variables; for example, the quality of communication might range from very poor to very good. Such behaviors do not necessarily occur continuously, but in a sample of people studied these variables range along a continuum from low to high.

Relationships

Most marriage and family research is concerned not so much with individual variables (like the age of marriage) but with relationships between them (age of marriage and marital stability). Researchers usually study how variables covary or vary together. When assessing relationships, a distinction is usually made between independent and dependent variables. The *dependent variable* is conceptualized as depending on (or being influenced by) the *independent variable*. This terminology is widely used across all of the sciences. In the example above, marital stability would be the dependent variable because it is thought to partially depend on, or be influenced by, the age at which people get married (the independent variable).

Sometimes variables in a relationship being studied can be conceptualized only one way. The age at marriage, for example, can influence marital stability, but marital stability cannot logically influence the age at which people marry; marital stability follows, comes after, or is partially dependent on the age at which people marry. Sometimes people think of such relationships as being *causal*. In order to infer that one variable causes another, (for example, variable X causes variable Y), three criteria are usually considered to be essential:

(1) covariation between variables (when X changes Y does, too);
(2) temporal priority of variable X before variable Y (X always occurs *before* Y); and
(3) the elimination of alternative explanations (ruling out other possible causes of Y).

Many relationships in marriage and family research do not meet all three criteria and can not be considered unequivocal causal statements. For example, some studies have proposed that marital satisfaction is partially dependent on the frequency of shared companionate activities of the husband and wife (Miller, 1976) or the quality of communication in marriage (Figley, 1973). However, it is equally plausible that satisfaction in marriage influences communication between spouses and the extent to which they share activities together.

Theories

Whereas concepts, variables, and relationships are the most fundamental elements of scientific thinking, theories include all of these elements. Theories summarize the explanatory and predictive principles in a field of study by characterizing the general patterns and regularities of individual phenomena. A theory can be defined as "a set of interrelated constructs, definitions, and propositions that presents a systematic view of phenomena by specifying relations among variables, with the purpose of explaining and predicting the phenomena" (Kerlinger, 1973: 9). More simply put, theories are general principles that summarize what we know about a particular set of relationships. In marriage and family studies, major efforts were made during the 1970s to develop and summarize theoretical principles (Burr, 1973; Burr et al., 1979).

STAGES IN THE RESEARCH PROCESS

The process of conducting research can be divided into stages, although in actual practice these often overlap and their boundaries are not sharply distinct. The number of stages identified also varies from one account to another. What is important, however, is that the logic of the sequence in research is understood. At a minimum, stages of the scientific method will include

(1) the idea, question, or problem;
(2) specific research questions or hypotheses;
(3) data collection and observations; and
(4) data analysis and interpretation.

To provide greater clarity, more specific stages of research are discussed in detail below.

Formulating the Problem

There is no single way of coming up with a researchable question or problem. Ideas might emerge from personal experiences and insights, from observing others, from studying professional literature, or in many other ways. Regardless of the source of the idea, the important task at the first stage is to move from a general idea or issue to a clearly defined question that will focus the research.

Writing out a research statement usually makes it clearer to oneself and to others what gap in knowledge is addressed by the study. Although the problem usually seems important to the investigator, it might seem "ho-hum," or a waste of time and money to significant others (supervisors, taxpayers, and sponsors). For this reason the formal written statement of the research problem usually includes specific aims, rationale, and justification. Part of the rationale might be given in explaining the problem to be studied, but the justification specifically tells *why* the research needs to be done at all. The research might be justified because it helps to fill a gap in knowledge, or because answering the question(s) and solving the problem(s) would have practical benefits for the sponsor or for society.

Specifying Hypotheses or Objectives

Hypotheses are testable conjectural statements about supposed relationships between variables: hypotheses are the link between theoretical ideas and empirical data. A well-written hypothesis states the expected relationships between variables so specifically that after the data are analyzed it will be clear whether the hypothesis has been disproven or supported. In actual practice, researchers sometimes are guided by incipient or unstated hypotheses in their minds. In most cases, though, researchers still seem to favor the traditional practice of writing out testable statements about the expected relationships between variables. This is likely to be required by some sponsors and for those who are conducting their first studies.

There are basically two kinds of hypotheses. The *substantive hypothesis,* or *alternative hypothesis,* states the anticipated relationship in declarative sentence form, just as the researcher expects to find it. For example, "Those who marry when they are younger than 20 are more likely to divorce than those who marry when they are older." Or stated differently, "There is an inverse relationship between the age of marriage and the probability of divorce." The second kind of hypothesis is called the *null hypothesis,* meaning the hypothesis of no difference or no relationship. For example, "There is no difference in divorce rates of those who marry at age 19 or younger and those who marry at older ages." Philosophically speaking, it is not possible to prove or accept the substantive hypothesis, but it is possible to reject the null hypothesis. Consequently, after data are collected, they are analyzed to test the null hypotheses. The substantive hypothesis that the researcher is usually most interested in is evaluated indirectly by testing the null hypothesis statistically.

Not all research, however, is of the hypothesis-testing kind. In some cases so little is known about an issue that the investigator might choose to do an exploratory or descriptive study rather than testing relationships between variables that are only dimly understood. When little is known about an issue, investigators can hardly expect to state informed hypotheses. Even when hypotheses cannot be stated it is still possible to state clear objectives for the research to be conducted. Specifically stated objectives or hypotheses will guide the research toward accomplishing what the investigator wants to do and prevent aimless wandering.

Choosing a Research Design

The *research design* is the overall plan and structure of a study. The most interesting and important research questions and the most clearly stated hypotheses or objectives are of little value unless some design can be devised for bringing relevant data to bear on the issue. The governing principle here is that the choice of research design depends on what the researcher wants to investigate. The researcher's approach should be based on a thoughtful consideration of the alternative strategies for investigating the research questions that have been posed. Different approaches are usually possible and sometimes deliberately used in combination to produce a richer and more complete picture of results (Caplow et al., 1982). In many cases, however, one design would most adequately facilitate investigation of the research questions with maximum efficiency.

Take, for example, the research question, "In what proportion of marriages is the wife premaritally pregnant?" An investigator could ask people directly and estimate this, but such an approach would be highly suspect because of the sensitivity of the question. An alternative, and probably more appropriate design, would be to match marriage and birth dates on official records (Christensen, 1963). In this example, asking personal questions and examining official records are alternative research designs. Issues of research design will be discussed more fully in Chapter 2.

Devising or Refining Measurement

Measurement enables the researcher to calibrate the characteristics, differences, changes, effects, and the strength of relationships. What the investigator finds out from the study will depend on how well the variables have been measured. Measurement requires clear thinking to link the concepts to observations. Is the measure to be used inclusive enough? Clear enough? Does it mean exactly what is intended by the major concepts of the study? Can it be used accurately and consistently? Because accurate measurement is complicated and difficult to achieve, it is often wise to use existing measuring instruments and procedures. When previously developed measures are not available, then devising and refining one's own measurement instruments will be an especially crucial stage of the research process. Marriage and family measurement is covered in detail in Chapter 3.

Selecting Subjects

Deciding who or what to study will usually be an integral part of the decision about the most appropriate kind of research design. Actually, choosing the subjects is likely to depend on a complex series of related decisions: Do the subjects chosen (the sample) need to represent any particular larger group (the population) to which the investigator wants to generalize the results? Do the data need to be collected from the observation of subjects or the self-report of respondents? Are data already available that might answer the research question without having to collect primary data? How large a sample will be needed? How should the sample be selected? As in all of the previous stages of research, choices at this stage depend on what one is trying to find out. Depending on the research questions various sample characteristics such as age, race, marital status, and other variables might be important definers of the sample to be selected.

Collecting Data

Data collection is the process of actually acquiring the empirical data that will (it is hoped) provide answers to the questions that initiated the research. This is the stage of observation or applying measurements. Often viewed as the least intellectual or conceptual part of the study, it is the most intensive, direct, and routine stage. Figuratively speaking, data collection gets one's hands dirty. Up to this point in the study, most of the work is mental and preparatory. When collecting data the investigator is actually in the field (or lab) observing or measuring the variables of interest. As discussed in Chapter 5, many techniques have been devised for obtaining and maintaining cooperation of those being studied, for maximizing the efficiency of the data collection process, and for maximizing the quality of the data obtained.

Reducing and Analyzing Data

Once the data have been collected they must be organized in some logical manner. This is the stage in which the data are cleaned up and arranged. Sometimes the original or raw data need to be transformed into scores of various kinds. In any case, the data must be tabulated or analyzed in such a way that they will be interpretable, and directly bear on the research questions that were posed. Sometimes simple analyses can be performed by hand, but with the advent of computers most analyses are now performed by machines (directed by researchers, of course). Data are nearly always converted into machine-readable forms so that even huge files can be stored and complex analyses can be performed through the use of high-speed computers. As discussed in Chapter 6, data entry, manipulation, and analysis have become highly technical aspects of most contemporary marriage and family research.

Interpreting Findings
and Drawing Conclusions

After the data have been analyzed the findings need to be interpreted. What do the results mean? What are the plausible explanations for the results obtained? Have the hypotheses been supported or refuted? How do the findings differ from or support previous research? If the study has been well designed, the investigator will be confident enough to draw some conclusions after data analysis. More often than not, however, weaknesses of the study design, measurement, sampling, and so on will limit the extent to which conclusions can be reached. It is frequently the case that unanticipated results or variations from what was expected will generate new hypotheses to be tested. Because new hypotheses are often generated by a study, research is commonly viewed as a circular process that both begins and ends with researchable questions.

SUMMARY

Marriage and family research addresses empirical rather than normative questions. Policymakers, researchers, and the public generally accept the scientific approach as an appropriate and useful way of acquiring reliable empirical information about important marriage and family phenomena.

The debate about hard and soft sciences is far from over and it involves many issues. The position taken in this book is that studying human beings and their relationships in marriages and families is considerably different than studying rocks, atomic particles, or viruses, but many of the scientific methods and principles are still useful.

Family research is conducted with the primary goals of describing, explaining, predicting, and (sometimes) controlling marriage and family behavior. Objectivity of research procedures and their public nature make it possible for different investigators to refute previous conclusions or to achieve similar results (replication), thus strengthening the believability of empirical generalizations and theories.

Some of the fundamental elements of scientific thought are concepts, variables, and the relationships between them. Theories are integrative sets of concepts and propositions about their relationships; they constitute the explanatory and predictive general principles of a scientific field.

The process of conducting research usually begins with an idea or problem that can become a researchable question. A research design is devised that will allow the appropriate data to be collected, and observations are obtained. Data analysis and interpretation lead to some answers or conclusion(s) about the questions that initiated the research. Often new questions are raised as well.

Empirically based knowledge about marriages and families is important for its own sake and for its practical benefits to society. Acquiring knowledge is a worthwhile end in itself, and the understanding it allows makes it possible to have empirically informed prevention, intervention, and public policies.

KEY CONCEPTS

Normative questions
Empirical questions
Science; hard and soft; physical, natural, social; family
Research, basic and applied
Goals of science
    Description
    Explanation
    Prediction
    Control
Objectivity
Replication

Empirical generalizations
Concepts
Variables
    Categorical variable
    Continuous variable
Relationships
    Independent variable
    Dependent variable
    Causality
Theory
Stages of research
    Idea or problem
    Specific questions or hypotheses
    Data collection, observations
    Interpretation, conclusions

CHAPTER

2

Research Design

Research design is the plan, structure, and strategy of investigation conceived so as to obtain answers to research questions . . .

Kerlinger (1973: 300)

AFTER THE RESEARCH PROBLEM is conceptualized clearly and the research questions have been formulated and refined, the next logical step is deciding how the study will be conducted. How can the study best be "designed" to answer the specific questions? Research design is a matter of planning out or deciding on the structure and approach to be taken in the research.

For most marriage or family research questions alternative approaches could be used. However, there are advantages and disadvantages to each design. In selecting a design and working out its details there are two major considerations: (1) fit—the design should provide for the clearest and most unequivocal answer possible, and (2) efficiency—the design should be as practical and resource efficient as possible.

The first consideration is that the research design must *fit* the problem; the most sophisticated design is of no value if it produces data

29

that are not directly relevant to the research questions of interest. Sometimes an investigator becomes so devoted to a particular design that it dictates the kinds of research questions he or she studies. The point of view taken in this chapter is much more eclectic; there are many useful alternative designs—each with their own strengths and weaknesses—that can be used for family research. Choosing among them, or tailoring something unique, should be based on fitting specific research questions. When the study is completed, the results should be clearly interpretable with a minimum of competing or alternative explanations for the results obtained.

The second major consideration, *practical efficiency,* means that designing a study must also take into account the time, money, and skill required. Sometimes the ideal design for studying the question at hand would be more expensive or time consuming than the investigator's resources will allow. The research to be conducted also must be within the skills possessed by the investigator, or at least within the range of skills that can be acquired by reasonable consultation or collaboration. In sum, the research design should not only *fit* the question being posed, enabling the investigator to draw clear conclusions, but it must also be *practical* from the standpoint of the financial, time, and skill resources required.

KINDS OF RESEARCH DESIGNS

There are various ways of classifying social and behavioral research designs, and each kind of design is used in marriage and family studies. One of the broadest ways of classifying types of research is into *qualitative* and *quantitative* approaches. Qualitative research is based on the nonnumerical examination and analysis of observations, interviews, or written materials. Some of the best known "classics" in family studies relied on qualitative analysis of in-depth interviews to identify types of marriage relationships (Cuber and Harroff, 1965). Probably less than 10% of marriage and family research is qualitative, however, although some have predicted or called for its increasing use (LaRossa and Wolf, 1985). Such a large majority of marriage and family research is quantitative (based on numerical measurement and analysis) that the dichotomous distinction is not a very instructive way of explaining research design. For purposes of this chapter, research designs are divided into the following categories:

(1) exploratory,
(2) descriptive,
(3) developmental,
(4) experimental, and
(5) correlational.

Exploratory Studies

Exploratory studies, as the name implies, are carried out when little is known about an area or issue. When basic facts about the phenomena of interest are completely absent or largely lacking, an investigator might not be able to state specific hypotheses about the relationships between variables. Most importantly, if hypotheses are based on scant theoretical or empirical precedent, they are likely to be trivial or misguided. In exploratory research a qualitative approach is likely to be taken because more precise quantitative measurement might be premature. For all these reasons, an exploratory approach is most appropriate. For example, when very little was known about family violence, Gelles (1974) conducted mostly qualitative unstructured interviews in families with domestic violence records.

The purpose of exploratory research is to generate ideas about, and insights into, a relatively little-understood issue. Often the results of an exploratory study will be the generation of more precise research questions or testable hypotheses, but this is not necessarily the case. Sometimes an exploratory study is done to find out if a more rigorous study would be feasible, and, if so, what specific questions should be pursued and what procedures should be followed. Although an exploratory study might be an end in itself as an investigator follows his or her emerging ideas, if it is well done it is likely to be followed eventually—perhaps even by someone else—by more systematic and theoretically guided research.

Some people regard exploratory studies as hardly worth doing (usually as compared to the "better" kind of research that they conduct). Again, however, the key criterion in selecting a research design is its fit to the problem or question at hand. Perhaps one reason for the relatively low regard for exploratory studies is that they sometimes are entered into without any plan or structure to the process of investigation. By its very nature, an exploratory study is likely to be somewhat less structured than other types of research; it must remain flexible in order to pursue leads and procedures that emerge in the process of investigation. This does not, however, mean that an exploratory study should proceed blindly and without direction.

Several activities can guide and give direction to exploratory research (Selltiz et al., 1976: 92-101). These include a thorough review of related literatures and interviews with people who have first-hand experience with the issue. Of course, the literature review is an essential part of every study. Interviews with experienced persons might focus on individuals who are selected for their potential to provide first-hand, relevant, and contrasting insights about the phenomena of interest. A variety of knowledgeable respondents might be interviewed, such as parents, siblings, relatives, friends, and agency professionals (police officers, social workers, teachers). A related strategy for guiding exploratory research is to focus on individuals who might have particularly salient viewpoints because they are strangers or newcomers, marginal individuals, those in transition, and so on.

Although exploratory studies are sometimes criticized, they fill an important need in family research. The more subjective, flexible, approach of the exploratory design is not well suited to testing hypotheses and drawing firm conclusions, but a well-executed exploratory study can evoke, identify, and refine ideas about research questions.

Descriptive Research

Occasionally exploratory and descriptive research are grouped together because some exploratory studies are written up descriptively. However, many descriptive marriage and family studies are not exploratory. Exploratory and descriptive research are not synonymous because exploratory studies are undertaken to *find out* what the important variables and issues are, whereas descriptive studies begin with specific variables and seek to *describe them* or their distribution among a certain group of people. Second, whereas exploratory studies maintain considerable flexibility and rely heavily on subjective insights, descriptive studies aim for completeness and accuracy and must, therefore, be more structured to guard against errors and biases. The United States Census is not an exploratory study, but it is a massive description (an enumeration, actually) of the population. Census data are used widely to describe marriage and family characteristics such as family size and composition. Using U.S. Census data it is possible to state, for example, that one family in five was headed by a single parent in 1980. Similarly, public opinion polls and family-focused descriptive surveys use specific structured questions to describe accurately attitudes and behaviors of interest to marriage and family researchers.

A descriptive study typically proceeds much like the steps or phases of the research process presented in Chapter 1. That is, once the research questions about changes over time (Aldous, 1978; Hill and of the scientific process are followed; specific procedures of data collection are chosen and measurement refined; the population and sample characteristics are specified; and data are collected, analyzed, and interpreted. Because each of these stages are common to all research, subsequent chapters will discuss them in detail.

At this point it should be readily apparent that the success of a descriptive study depends heavily on the care and precision with which it is designed and carried out. Descriptive studies are not limited to any one method of data collection. For example, descriptive marriage and family studies have included census and historical document analysis to describe how families have changed over long periods of time (Laslett, 1971; Seward, 1978), intensive and continuous in-home observations to describe the internal dynamics of family life (Kantor and Lehr, 1975), and personal interviews to estimate the amount and kinds of violence in the home (Straus et al., 1980).

Designs for
Studying Developmental Changes

The study of development is centrally concerned with understanding changes over time. Much of the research in child development, developmental psychology, and human development focuses on how individuals change. Similarly, marriage and family scholars often study research questions about changes over time (Aldous, 1978; Hill and Mattessich, 1979). What, for example, is the relationship between the length of marriage and its qualities? How does the interaction between spouses (or siblings, or parents and children) change over time?

Longitudinal research designs are those in which observations or assessments are made on the same subjects more than once so that naturally occurring changes can be detected. With two or more observations of the same individuals, changes in their scores can be calculated directly. This is a highly simplified characterization of longitudinal designs, but their key defining characteristic should be clear; the same subjects are measured at two or more points in time so that naturally occurring changes can be detected.

The simplest and most common form of longitudinal design is one in which the subjects are measured either at regular (e.g., yearly) intervals or before and after especially important developmental events (e.g., puberty, marriage, childbirth, retirement, etc.). Sometimes studies of the same subjects over time are referred to as *panel studies,* because repeated observations or measures are taken of the same group or panel of individuals or families. A prominent example is the panel study of income dynamics among 5000 families who have been studied annually since 1968 by James Morgan and others at Michigan's Institute for Social Research. A longer term and more psychological example is the Berkeley Longitudinal Growth Study that focuses on individual change. These longitudinal data have been used for numerous analyses of individual, marital, and family change (Elder, 1974; Liker and Elder, 1983).

An alternative to longitudinal design for the study of development is the cross-sectional study (Hill, 1964). In a *cross-sectional design,* data are collected only once on subjects of different ages, and the inference is made that age differences in the behaviors of interest have resulted from changes in subjects or marriages or families as they aged. This strategy is used frequently in child development studies. For example, Bowerman and Kinch (1959) wanted to know how children's orientations to peers and parents changed over time, from middle childhood to adolescence. Rather than following the same group (or panel) of children over these years, they asked questions about peer and parent orientations to children of different ages. Although their data were based on responses of different children at each age, they concluded that peer orientation increases, and parent orientation decreases, as children grow older. Using a similar cross-sectional approach, a researcher interviewed spouses who have been married between one and six years to study how the frequency and meaning of sexual relations changed during the early years of marriage (Greenblat, 1983).

Studies about changes in marital perceptions and qualities over time have used both longitudinal and cross-sectional designs. One of the most ambitious longitudinal marriage studies was begun by Ernest Burgess in 1939. Beginning with 1000 couples, the investigators assessed couple adjustment and partner perceptions during engage-

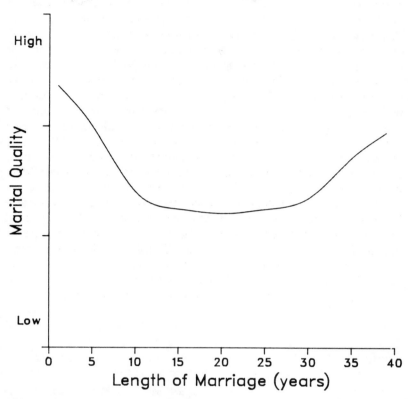

NOTE: Differences in marital satisfaction and adjustment generalized from cross-sectional studies comparing spouses married different lengths of time (Figley, 1973; Miller, 1976; Rollins and Cannon, 1974; Rollins and Feldman, 1970); decreases generalized from longitudinal data showing changes between being childless and having an infant (Belsky et al., 1983; Feldman, 1971; Miller and Sollie, 1980; Ryder, 1973), and over the first 20 years of marriage (Dizard, 1968; Pineo, 1961).

Figure 2.1 Shape of Relationship Between Marital Qualities and Length of Marriage

ment, after 3 years of marriage, and during the twentieth year of marriage. Observing that marital adjustment of both husbands and wives decreased over time, Pineo (1961) wrote about "disenchantment in the later years of marriage." Using cross-sectional designs many studies have been done comparing qualities of marriage at different durations of marriage, or stages of family development (Miller, 1976; Rollins and Cannon, 1974; Rollins and Feldman, 1970). Figure 2.1 shows the general shape of the relationship between length of marriage and marital quality.

The study of marriage initiated by Burgess in 1939 provides a good example of the limitations of the long-term longitudinal approach (Burgess and Wallin, 1953). The study began with 1000 couples but only 666 were located and reinterviewed after 3 years, and only 400 were included in the 20-year follow-up (Dizard, 1968; Pineo, 1961). A major problem of long-term longitudinal studies has been attrition of subjects and the research staff, in addition to expense. Recently, however, large, sophisticated, and well-funded projects have reported 85%-90% retention of participants throughout longitudinal family studies lasting up to 20 years (Call et al., 1982; Freedman et al., 1980; Thornton et al., 1982).

Another alternative to using either a long-term longitudinal or cross-sectional approach is the short-term longitudinal study. In a short-term longitudinal study the same subjects are measured at least twice, but over a relatively brief period of time (several months or years as opposed to the life span). For example, several short-term longitudinal studies of marital qualities have been conducted, showing slight to modest decreases in the perceived quality of marriage after the birth of the first baby (Belsky et al., 1985; Miller and Sollie, 1980; Ryder, 1973).

Experimental Designs for Studying Induced Changes

Although the vast majority of marriage and family research is nonexperimental, it is important to understand the logic of experiments and their importance for certain kinds of research questions. The experiment is the preferred design in most of the "hard sciences," and it is occasionally the preferred design for answering empirical questions about a particular marriage or family issue.

Experiments are designed especially to allow an investigator to infer functional or causal relationships between independent and dependent variables. This is because *an experiment is a study in which the investigator manipulates, applies,* or *introduces the independent variable (or treatment) and observes its effect on the dependent variable.* When the research question is a causal one, and if manipulation of the independent variable is under the control of the investigator (this is usually the big *if* in marriage and family research), then an experiment would probably be the method of choice.

For example, anecdotal and impressionistic evidence abounds that there is a social stigma against single adults, and especially against divorcées. Suppose a researcher wanted to find out how marital status (independent variable) affected how individuals are perceived (dependent variable); this could be done—with a little ingenuity—experimentally. For example, in one study (Etaugh and Malstrom, 1981) subjects were asked to rate the personal traits of an individual described in a paragraph. Subjects rated the person after reading exactly the same description, except that marital status (married, widowed, divorced, never married) was varied ("manipulated") by the experimenter. In other words, some subjects rated a single person, some a married person, and so on. On the 20 traits that were rated, married individuals were generally rated more favorably than all groups of unmarried individuals, and widows were viewed more favorably than either divorced or never-married singles on 15 of 20 items (Etaugh and Malstrom, 1981).

Many experimental designs include more than one assessment or observation of the same subjects (pre- and posttests), as a longitudinal study does. However, the reason for doing an experiment is to *induce* or to *cause* changes by manipulating an independent variable. Longitudinal designs, by contrast, study uninduced maturation and historical changes themselves (development) as the phenomena of interest.

There are many types of experimental designs, but their common element is the manipulation of the independent variable. In other words, a treatment is given and its effects observed. However, interpreting results based only on a treatment and a posttest observation , or even pre- and posttest observations of the same group, is hazardous because there are many plausible alternative explanations for the results obtained. Perhaps changes within the subjects (maturation) occurred unrelated to the treatment, or changes occurred external to the subjects (history) that affected their posttest scores independently of the treatment. Suppose, for example, that engaged couples were pretested and then given a communication training treatment prior to marriage; six months later they scored higher or better on their posttest communication scores. Improved communication posttest scores could be due to the communication treatment, but they could also be due to naturally occurring changes in the couples (maturation) or to a church or community emphasis on improving young couples' readiness for marriage (history), and not because of the treatment program at all. Cook and Campbell (1979) classified such inadequate approaches as "preexperimental" designs and argued that a prerequisite for a "true" group experimental design is that there be both control and experimental groups that are equivalent (or that can be assumed to be equivalent) before any treatment is given.

Matching subjects with similar characteristics in control and experimental groups has often been used to compose groups that are supposed to be equivalent, but many authorities argue that this approach is seriously flawed (Campbell and Stanley, 1963; Kerlinger, 1979). Matching subjects on one, two, or several variables that are thought to be important to the research issue at hand might be feasible, but there are innumerable potentially confounding variables on which subjects should perhaps be matched. Sometimes even variables that the investigators have not thought about beforehand turn out to complicate interpretation of the results. For these reasons, successful matching is questionable.

The principle of *randomness*—meaning no order or rule or pattern—is used in research in two very important ways, namely random assignment and random selection (Campbell and Stanley, 1963). Random selection will be discussed in the chapter on sampling; selecting subjects randomly is very important to *external validity*, or being able to generalize results from the sample to a larger population of interest. *Random assignment* (also called *randomization*) is the most important principle of group composition to assure *internal validity* in experimental research. If subjects are assigned to control and experimental groups by a random process, then characteristics of the subjects that might otherwise have confounded the results will be randomly distributed in the control and experimental groups. When random assignment can be used, it is the most powerful way of establishing preexperimental group equivalence. In the realities of everyday research, however, random assignment of subjects to groups is sometimes impossible (subjects might be in existing groups or classes over which the experimenter can have no control). In these situations alternative quasi- or nonexperimental designs must be used to minimize threats to internal and external validity (Cook and Campbell, 1979).

Using the symbolic notations of Campbell and Stanley (1963), three of the best known true experimental designs are shown in Table 2.1. In this table R indicates that subjects have been randomly assigned to achieve group equivalence before treatment begins, X represents the exposure of a group to an experimental treatment, and O indicates an observation or measurement of the dependent variable. Xs and Os in

TABLE 2.1
Basic Group Experimental Designs

(1)	Pretest – Posttest Control Group Design			
	R	O	X	O
	R	O		O
(2)	Posttest Only Control Group Design			
	R		X	O
	R			O
(3)	Solomon Four-Group Design			
	R	O	X	O
	R	O		O
	R		X	O
	R			O

NOTE: Notation system from Campbell and Stanley (1963); R = random assignment; O = observation; X = treatment; left to right equals time dimension.

the same row are applied to the same persons, and the left-to-right dimension indicates temporal order; Xs and Os vertical to each other occur simultaneously.

All three experimental designs shown in Table 2.1 control for the major threats to internal validity (see Campbell and Stanley, 1963, Table 1). Using these designs, a strong inference is justified that the treatment X is the cause of differences in group posttest scores. With design 1, for example, changes within (maturation) or external (history) to subjects might occur between pre- and posttest, but these effects should be manifest equally in the control and experimental groups because they were composed by random assignment. The only way in which the groups should differ systematically is that one was exposed to the experimental treatment X and the other was not. The effect of testing (giving a pretest) should also affect both groups similarly in design 1 and might possibly be reflected to an unknown extent in their posttest scores. The effect of testing can be eliminated by using design 2, which simply does away with the pretest; if the groups are randomly composed and large enough, there should be no need of pretesting. Design 3, the Solomon four-group design, combines the preceding two designs, making it possible to actually assess the effect of pretesting by comparing groups 1 and 3, and 2 with 4.

The vast majority of experimental studies in the human sciences are group experiments; that is, the independent variable is manipulated (the treatment is given) to all subjects in the experimental group and its effects are assessed by comparing the average group score on the dependent variable with the average score of subjects in the control group who did not receive the treatment. However, experiments with single subjects are not only possible but sometimes desirable (Hersen and Darlow, 1976). The logic of single subject experiments is analogous to group designs, at least the logic of manipulating the independent variable and observing its effects.

In single-case experimental designs, the initial period of observation involves the repeated measurement of the natural frequency of the targeted behavior (dependent variable) under study. This naturally occurring frequency of the targeted behavior is referred to as *baseline*, and it serves as a standard by which the subsequent levels of the targeted behavior can be compared. For example, a baseline observation might simply record the frequency of a parent's yelling at or striking a child. A minimum of three points of observation are required to establish a pattern in the behavior, and a general rule is that baseline should be continued until a stable pattern is evident. Two basic kinds of single-subject experimental designs that are used to assess the effect of a treatment on individual behavior are shown in Figure 2.2.

In a reversal design (see figure 2.2A), the treatment (for example, relaxation therapy) is applied after baseline observation of the targeted behavior (e.g., parental yelling). During baseline 2 the treatment is removed or withdrawn to see if the behavior "reverses" or returns to its former (baseline) level. The relaxation therapy might be reapplied in treatment 2 to establish a functional relationship between the treatment and the parent's negative behavior. Figure 2.2A illustrates a case in which treatment 1 reduced the target behavior by more than half, but the behavior returned to its former level when the treatment was removed.

An alternative to the single-subject reversal design is the multiple baseline (see Figure 2.2B). It is most useful for studying relationships in which the treatment cannot or should not be withdrawn for either ethical or practical reasons. With baselines established for the several behaviors of the subject, the investigator applies the experimental treatment to one of the behaviors and looks for a change in it, perhaps noting little or no change in the other behaviors. (An important assumption of this design is that the targeted behaviors are independent of each other.) For example, behaviorally oriented clinical psychologists might use a multiple baseline approach to study the treatment of a teenager with severe behavior problems (screaming,

A. Reversal Design

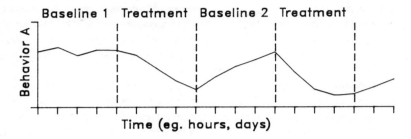

B. Multiple Baseline Design

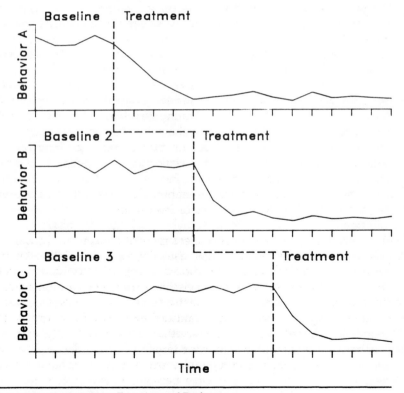

Figure 2.2   Single-Subject Experimental Designs

hitting, pants-wetting, etc.). The first targeted behavior (screaming) could be treated by an aversive stimulus of some kind (cold water sprayed in the face). When the targeted behavior is reduced, another behavior (hitting) then begins to be treated also until it subsides, and so on.

Correlational Designs

Correlational studies take their name from the statistics used to measure the degree of association or correlation between variables being studied. Correlational studies assess the degree to which two or more variables covary or go together. For example, a great many studies have been done relating or correlating family size with academic achievement and intelligence. In contrast to exploratory studies and descriptive research, correlational studies set out to examine specific relationships between variables.

Correlational studies are like experimental studies in that both assess relationships between two or more variables. The major difference is that correlational designs are used to study relationships between variables that are not under the control of the investigator. Researchers can only do correlational studies about the effects of family size, birth order, marital status, and so on. In other words, correlational designs are used to assess relationships in which the independent variable cannot or should not be experimentally manipulated. Correlational research is often termed *ex post facto* (meaning after the fact), because the independent variables (such as sex, race, marital status, family size) have already had their effects.

The majority of marriage and family studies are correlational or ex post facto. One reason for this is that the field has moved toward a scientific orientation that values going beyond description to the empirical testing of relationships. At the same time, however, most marriage and family research questions are extremely difficult or impossible to design as experiments because it is not feasible to randomly assign subjects to treatment and control groups or to manipulate the independent variable and observe its effects. It appears that marriage and family research is dominated by correlational designs because they fit the research questions of interest to scholars in this field.

The correlational approach can be used with several methods of data collection (observations, questionnaires, interviews, etc.). The key difference is in the research questions that are asked and, sometimes, in how the study is conducted. The conduct of an experiment and an ex post facto study are quite different (manipulating variables versus correlating them). The key difference between descriptive and correlational studies lies not with the procedure but in the kinds of research questions asked, which determines how the data are analyzed and interpreted. In fact, the variables included, the measurement, and data collection procedures can be identical in a descriptive study and in a correlational study, but variables will be correlated in the latter.

One of the most rapidly increasing ways of doing correlational research is by reanalyzing data that were originally collected in another study. *Secondary analyses* are analyses of data for purposes that were not originally intended and usually are performed by persons other than those who collected them (Hyman, 1972; Stewart, 1984). Secondary analyses of existing data have made important contributions to marriage and family studies. Some recent examples include the analysis of cohort and period effects on individual and family development (Elder, 1974); analyses of family size and composition related to children's characteristics (Blake, 1981; Kidwell, 1982); the effects of children on marriage quality (Glenn and McLanahan, 1982) and on the probability of divorce (Cherlin, 1977). Such secondary analyses can be based on data that were primarily descriptive survey or census data. For example, the General Social Surveys conducted by the National Opinion Research Center (NORC) contain a large amount of data that can be used simply to describe marriages and families, but these data can also be used in correlational studies (Davis, 1978). Reiss and colleagues (1980), for example, used the NORC data archive to study the relationships between extramarital sexual permissiveness and variables like religiosity, gender equality, premarital sexual permissiveness, and marital happiness.

DESIGN-STRENGTHENING TECHNIQUES

Some techniques to strengthen research designs already have been introduced (for example, random assignment to increase internal validity in experiments and random selection to increase generalizability). A few of the many other ways to strengthen research design are presented briefly in this section.

An investigator might hypothesize that a father's presence at his infant's delivery would be related to the father's displays of interest, affection, and attachment when he later interacted with the baby. Some people might even think that being present at delivery *increases* positive fathering behaviors. In theory the independent variable (father's presence at delivery) could be manipulated by randomly assigning some fathers to be present and others absent and seeing what effect this treatment had on the dependent variable (father's behavior). Practically and ethically speaking, of course, a true group experiment of this type would be virtually impossible, so less conclusive designs have been used in which fathers' voluntary presence at delivery was related to fathering behaviors (Miller and Bowen, 1982). If, however, observers who rated fathering behaviors knew in advance which fathers had been present at delivery, this would pose a serious threat to the integrity of the study. Observers who know the research question being investigated and which fathers had been present might consciously or unconsciously fudge or rate the fathers' behaviors in the expected direction. In this case, design-strengthening techniques would entail having the observers of father behavior unaware or *blind* to the purpose of the research, or at least blind to whether or not fathers had been present during delivery (Miller and Bowen, 1982).

On the other hand, subjects who know what researchers want or expect in a study sometimes fudge their behavior or responses accordingly. In studies where this could be a problem the research design would be strengthened by having *subjects* blind to the purposes of the research. In a *double-blind* study both research personnel and subjects are kept ignorant of the hypotheses or of what treatment has been received. In experimental studies control subjects are sometimes given a *placebo* (a phony treatment) so that their reactions can be compared with those who receive the treatment being studied.

Some of the above examples of design-strengthening techniques are special cases of strategies used to cope with the general problem of reactivity. *Reactivity means that subjects who are aware of being studied react differently than they ordinarily would, thus affecting and obscuring the research results.* Research designs are strengthened to the extent that reactivity is controlled for or reduced. Sometimes the procedures and measures used can be unobtrusive or nonreactive because they do not require the respondent's cooperation or, perhaps, even their awareness (Webb et al., 1966). When subjects are aware of being studied the design-strengthening techniques mentioned can sometimes be used.

KEY PRINCIPLES IN RESEARCH DESIGN

One key principle of research design is to measure the variables in the substantive hypothesis, both independent and dependent variables, in such a manner that relationships can be detected. In designing an experiment, the treatment must be planned so that it will be powerful enough to have an effect. That is, the experimenter must make the experimental variable(s) really vary. In correlational research the logic remains the same; if the independent and dependent variables are not measured so that they vary sufficiently there is little chance of detecting a relationship between them. For example, in a correlational study of the relationship between social class (the independent variable) and physical punishment in child rearing, it would not be appropriate to use a sample of mostly middle-class parents because the social class variable would have such a limited range of variation. Neither would it be appropriate to use a very rough or crude measure of social class in a more diverse sample. If a relationship exists between the variables being studied, it can only be found to the extent that the variables have been measured appropriately. This can be done by making experimental treatments powerful enough to show up or by measuring nonexperimental variables in such a way that they are allowed a full range of variation.

Not all of the variation in the dependent variable comes from the independent variable(s) being studied; some of the variation in scores comes from just noise or error. Therefore, another important principle is to minimize the error variance, which means that the variability in scores that arises through random fluctuations (error) must be reduced as much as possible. Random variance enters a study through individual differences, through transient lapses of attention, fatigue, guessing, coding and data preparation errors, and through measurement error due to low reliability of the measuring instrument or procedure. It is essential to reduce error variance as much as possible to give the variance due to the variables of interest a chance to show up.

TABLE 2.2

A Summary of the MAXMINCON Principle

MAX – Maximize the variation of the sustantive variables.
- (a) have the experimental treatment(s) strong enough to show up, or;
- (b) measure independent variables so that they have maximum variation.

MIN – Minimize the error variance.
- (a) Use a design that identifies variance due to individual differences.
- (b) Reduce errors of measurement through controlled conditions and quality control procedures.
- (c) Increase the reliability of the measures used to collect data.

CON – Control extraneous variables.
- (a) Eliminate by means of homogenous sampling of subjects.
- (b) Randomize; randomly assign subjects and treatments in experiments.
- (c) Match subjects.
- (d) Build the extraneous variable into the design.
- (e) Use statistical controls to remove effects of extraneous variables.

SOURCE: Adapted from Kerlinger (1973) to apply to both experimental and correlational designs.

If error variance is large in proportion to the total variance, then the relationships being studied will not be discernable.

A third important principle is that extraneous variables must be controlled. Extraneous variables are potentially contaminating variables that must be minimized, nullified, or their effect isolated by the research design. Variance in the dependent variables that comes from these extraneous variables must be reduced to zero, or it must be possible to separate analytically its effects from the variance of the substantive independent variables under study. One way of controlling extraneous variables is through homogenous sampling; subjects can be chosen so that they are matched on the variable to be controlled. For example, eliminating race as an extraneous variable by studying only whites reduces how widely the results can be generalized. The best (but not always practical) way of controlling extraneous variance in experimental studies is to randomly assign subjects to groups. A related but much less satisfactory way of controlling extraneous variance in group comparisons is to match subjects in each group on the variable(s) of concern. Alternatively, the potentially contaminating extraneous variable can be eliminated by building it into the design so that both its direct effects and interaction effects can be ascertained. Extraneous variables are usually controlled for in correlational or ex post facto

Zeller, 1979; Zeller and Carmines, 1980) have recently suggested the more general definition of measurement given in the opening sentence of this chapter—namely, that measurement is the systematic process of linking abstract concepts to empirical indicators.

The explicit procedures, rules, or instructions for linking concepts and indicators are frequently referred to as *operational definitions*. Measurement rules or operational definitions describe the "operations" necessary to produce scores for those being studied. The concept of child attachment to a parent, for example, might be operationalized by counting proximity-seeking behaviors of children and distress behaviors when the parent leaves. Operational definitions specify how variables are to be measured, whereas measurement is the actual process of obtaining scores.

Sometimes a single item or observation produces adequate data to reflect the intended concept as accurately as it seems necessary to measure it. For example, a single question usually suffices to measure characteristics such as sex, race, age, number of children, years of marriage, and so on. However, measurement becomes immensely more complex when assessing attitudes, perceptions, and other "latent" or unobserved variables.

Single items are sometimes used to measure variables such as marital satisfaction (Rollins and Feldman, 1970), but more frequently single *items* are combined to form a *composite score*. The concept to be measured might consist of a single dimension (McIver and Carmines, 1981) or it might be multidimensional (Kruskal and Wish, 1978). For example, some studies of marital satisfaction use several items to measure the single dimension of satisfaction with marriage (Miller, 1976) but other investigators (Spanier, 1976) are more interested in measuring marital adjustment, including the several dimensions of consensus, cohesion, satisfaction, and so on. There is an important reason for using composite scores to measure complex constructs like satisfaction, cohesion, adjustment, attachment, and so on. Basically, a single item reflects only part of the meaning of such complex phenomena. Composite scores capture a more complete measure of the concept than a single item would. Using multiple-item composite scores increases both the measure's reliability and validity, as will be explained later in this chapter.

Indicant or *indicator* are nearly synonymous terms that stand for, reflect, or indicate part of a concept being measured. Typically, indicators are combined into an *index,* which provides the total or composite score for the construct being measured. Although the term *indicator* has more conceptual sensitivity than the conceptually barren term *item,* they frequently are used interchangeably. Also composed of multiple items, a *test* carries the additional connotation of measuring achievement, ability, or aptitude.

The term *scale* is also frequently used in reference to measurement, and it has several meanings. The scale sometimes means the range of possible responses, a kind of numerical continuum implied when saying that someone scored "off the scale." There are several common ways of scaling measurements. The simplest and most widely used is a summated rating scale, or a *Likert-type scale,* on which attitudes are indicated by marking a response ranging between "strongly agree" and "strongly disagree" (ISR Newsletter, 1981; Likert, 1932). *Guttmans's scaleogram analysis* procedures for creating cumulative unidimensional scales also have been used in marriage and family studies. A well-known example is Reiss's (1967) scale of premarital sexual permissiveness, which has been used in many tests of his theoretical formulations (Reiss and Miller, 1979). Recently, marriage and family scholars have employed the bipolar-adjective format of *semantic differential scales* (Osgood et al., 1957; Snider and Osgood, 1969) in having respondents evaluate their marriage and family experiences (Campbell et al., 1976; Gecas, 1971; Miller and Sollie, 1980). New scaling procedures are continuing to be developed (Lodge, 1981). Perhaps more commonly, the term *scale* has come to mean the measuring instrument itself (Maranell, 1974). Thus, there are scales or instruments to measure dyadic adjustment (Spanier, 1976), family adaptability and cohesion (Olson et al., 1982), and so on.

LEVELS OF MEASUREMENT

Marriage and family researchers need to understand levels of measurement because they have important implications for choosing the most appropriate statistical analyses. Some concepts are, by their very nature, *categorical;* we think of a person's sex, race, and marital status, for example, as being just one of a number of discrete categories. *Continuous variables* such as attachment, cohesion, or compatibility are not either/or, one-or-the-other phenomena, but they vary by degrees along a continuum. The values of continuous variables differ from each other by more gradual or subtle gradations, as opposed to being of a different category or type. Categorical and continuous variables are a useful and common way of describing kinds of measurement, but traditionally measurement has been classified into four levels: nominal, ordinal, interval, and ratio.

Nominal

Nominal means naming. There is no metric associated with variables at the nominal level of measurement; instead, the values of such variables are known by their names. And, in fact, "to name something ('nominal') is to put it into a category ('categorical')" (Kerlinger, 1973: 159). Sex is a nominal or categorical variable and the names of the sexes are male and female. These categories are different in kind, not in amount or degree. When numbers are assigned to categories in nominal measurement, the numbers are used for grouping purposes only (e.g., male = 1, female = 2) and they have no numerical meaning or properties (they cannot be ordered, added, etc.).

Ordinal

Measurement at the ordinal level means that it is possible to rank order subjects (or other units being assessed) by their scores on the variable being measured. At the nominal level of measurement it would be clearly inappropriate to say (because we assigned the number 2 to females) that women are a "higher" sex, or have "more" biological sex than men. However, if the concept being measured has an ordinal property it would be possible to rank order subjects. Assigning numbers to this rank ordering would have a logical meaning—spouses who reported more conflict in marriage would have higher scores than those who reported less. Note, however, that ordinal numbers indicate rank order and nothing more.

> The numbers do not indicate absolute quantities, nor do they indicate that the intervals between the numbers are equal. For instance, it cannot be assumed that because the numerals are equally spaced, the under-lying properties they represent are equally spaced. . . . There is also no way to know that any individual has *none* of the property being measured. Rank order scales are not equal interval scales, nor do they have absolute zero points [Kerlinger, 1973: 437].

Interval

At the interval level of measurement, as the name implies, there are equal intervals between points of measurement. The length of marriage in years or the number of children in a family are variables that have interval properties. The "distance" between points of measurement are equal; that is, the length of time between one and three years of marriage is the same as the length of time between 27 and 29 years of marriage (two years is two years anywhere along the scale). Similarly, the difference between having one and two children (one child) is the same as the difference between having two and three children (I must admit that a weary parent of three once attacked my logic on this, emphatically telling me that having three children most definitely is *not* just one more than two).

Ratio

Ratio variables not only have equal distances between points of measurement, but they also have an absolute zero point, which means that there is none of the property being measured. The examples provided to illustrate interval measurement (years married and number of children) are actually ratio variables because people can have zero children and be married zero years. The arithmetic operations of multiplication and division are inherently meaningful with ratio measurement (e.g., married *half* as long, or with *twice* as many children).

RELIABILITY

To say that a measuring instrument or process is reliable means that it is *consistent* or *dependable*. Reliability is the most fundamental measurement characteristic because unreliable measures produce results that are meaningless. Even worse than finding no meaning in the data, one of the major problems in social science research is the misinterpretation of unreliable data and drawing erroneous conclusions. There is no way around it: Reliable measurement is *absolutely essential* for research results to be meaningful.

Another way of understanding reliability is to view it as the opposite or reverse of measurement error. Although the goal is to achieve the best measurement possible, nothing is ever measured perfectly. There is almost always some error in measurement, and the more error, the lower the reliability. The total variance in a set of scores can be attributed to true differences plus variation caused by errors in measurement. In other words, reliability is the proportion of "true" variance to the total variance of the data produced by a measuring instrument. In sum, a measure is reliable to the extent that variability in a set of scores accurately reflects true differences between subjects on the characteristic being assessed. Anastasi (1976) has written that any reliability coefficient can be interpreted directly in terms of the percentage of score variance attributable to different sources. For example, a reliability coefficient of .85 means that 85% of the variance in test scores depends on true variance on the trait measured and 15% is due to error variance.

The reliability of measurement can be calculated in a variety of ways. Reliability coefficients are often expressed as correlation coefficients, with 1.00 indicating perfect reliability (which in practice is never attained). Although there are now several ways of computing reliability coefficients, they all have in common a central concern with the consistency or agreement between sets of scores. Measures of reliability can be grouped into two conceptual classes: (1) measures of stability and (2) measures of equivalence.

Stability of Measurement

If a measuring instrument is reliable it should produce similar or stable scores for subjects assessed over time (assuming that the characteristic or trait being measured has not changed). This type of reliability, called test-retest, is obtained by twice administering an identical test or measure and correlating scores obtained by the same subjects on the two administrations. The resulting correlation expresses how consistent or "stable" the measure is over time. Error variance in test-retest procedures corresponds to random fluctuations in the administration of the measure (distractions, different conditions, etc.) and to random variations in the subjects such as fatigue, stress, or illness.

Several critical issues with test-retest reliability are the *length of time between tests, remembering, reactivity,* and *developmental changes.* Generally speaking, the magnitude of test-retest correlations declines as the length of time between tests increases. Consequently, test-retest administrations are usually separated by only a few weeks, and rarely as long as 6 months (Anastasi, 1976). Of course, the longer the interval between tests, the less that subjects' remembering should be an issue in assessing reliability. Conversely, however, the longer the interval between tests, the more that real changes are likely to occur within the subjects.

Alternate or parallel forms are one way of avoiding the problem of subjects *remembering* questions or responses on the previous administration. Alternate forms tap the same content, containing different but exactly the same number of items with exactly the same instructions, format, and so on. Unfortunately, it is extremely difficult to construct alternate measures that produce virtually identical scores. If alternate forms were administered together, one right after the other, the correlation between the two sets of scores would reflect reliability or consistency across forms only (the equivalence notion of reliability). If the administrations of alternate forms are separated by some time interval, the correlation between scores reflects test-retest stability in measurement that is unaffected by memory.

Reactivity to measurement is a persistent question in test-retest estimates of reliability. For example, assessing a certain attitude might change the respondent's awareness or sensitivity in such a way that the attitude really does change in reaction to the first assessment. This is part of a larger and much debated problem with test-retest procedures, namely, real *developmental* changes in the subjects. Test-retest procedures assume, of course, that the measured characteristic has not changed between assessments. This is often a very questionable assumption. And, perhaps even more troublesome, there is no way to tease out how much test-retest score differences are due to changes in subjects true scores, and how much are due to unreliable measurement. Perhaps because of this problem, most recent attention to techniques for estimating instrument reliability have focused on equivalence rather than stability over time. Before turning to equivalence procedures, however, there is another kind of stability measure that should be mentioned.

Intrarater reliability is concerned with observer or rater stability. When human observers or coders are the measuring instruments, it is important to know that they remain consistent in their ratings over time. Especially in a study in which data are gathered for several weeks, months, or even years, the observers (as the measuring instrument) must remain consistent. It would be very easy for early and later ratings to differ because of observer boredom or carelessness. To the extent that raters are not consistent over time, score differences would be due to measurement error, not to true differences or changes in behavior. When the behaviors under study can be stored in some way (film, videotape, writing, etc.), intrarater reliability can be assessed by having raters periodically rescore subjects that they scored earlier. Their agreement or correspondence between earlier and later ratings (in correlation coefficients or percent agreement) are an important measure of intrarater reliability, or stability over time.

Equivalence of Measures

The equivalence notion of reliability has both general and specific meanings. At the most general level, equivalence estimates of reliability are all concerned with comparing the correspondence or agreement between component parts of the measuring instrument or procedure. *Split-half estimates* of reliability focus specifically on the equivalence between two halves of a test; other types of *internal consistency estimates* assess inter-item equivalence or how each item contributes to or detracts from the total reliability of a measure; *interrater* reliability is concerned with the equivalence of ratings between two or more human "instruments" as they measure some variable. The specifics of these measures of equivalence are discussed separately.

Split-half estimates of reliability are attempts to assess the reliability of a measure administered only once. Two scores for each subject can be produced by dividing their responses to the instrument into halves. A number of formulas have been developed for computing coefficients, but basically the split-half reliability estimate relies on correlating subject's responses on the two halves of the instrument. A basic decision is how to group the items into two groups as there are so many possibilities. Comparing the equivalence of first and second halves of an instrument is usually not advisable because of fatigue or response bias in the second half, and so odd-even item splits have become most common.

Better estimates of internal consistency reliability have gradually replaced split-half procedures. Newer internal consistency estimates are based on examining the covariance of all items simultaneously rather than correlating two groups of items lumped together for split-half purposes. Because each item or indicator is evaluated separately in relation to the overall composite measure, internal consistency procedures are useful in initial scale development as well as in assessing how reliably an existing measuring instrument performed with a given sample. For example, if item analysis shows that one or more items are only weakly related to the overall scale, a better measure would result from leaving the weak item(s) out. The resulting composite scale would be more internally consistent. Probably the most widely used measure of internal consistency in the marriage and family field is coefficient "alpha" (Cronbach, 1951; Cronbach et al., 1972).

Interrater reliability is concerned with how consistent two (or more) raters are as measuring instruments. In the case of interrater reliability the measuring instrument being assessed consists of the raters or coders themselves. When measurement is based on the judgment of observers who code behavior into categories, the researcher must know if the measurement system (human raters) scores the phenomenon consistently. Consistency of each rater over time (intrarater stability) has already been described, but one must also know that multiple observers see the phenomena similarly (equivalence). Observers are usually trained until they agree substantially in their ratings (perhaps 85% or 90% agreement) before they actually begin collecting data that will be analyzed. Filmed or videotaped behavior sequences that can be replayed are particularly useful in training observers to attain high agreement. The terminology above refers to observers who score behavior from observations, but the principle of interrater reliability also applies to consistency between coders of other kinds of data (Cohen, 1960).

VALIDITY

The most common definition of validity is the extent to which a measuring instrument measures what it is intended to measure. To be useful in research, instruments must not only produce consistent results (reliability) but also reflect the intended construct (validity). An important distinction should be made here between reliability and validity. Reliability, or the lack of reliability, is a *characteristic of the measuring instrument itself*; validity is not a property of the instrument itself, but describes the appropriateness of the *use to which the measure is put.*

Thus, while reliability focuses on a particular property of empirical indicators—the extent to which they provide consistent results across repeated measurements—validity concerns the crucial relationship between concept and indicator [Carmines and Zeller, 1979: 12].

It is quite possible for a measure to be reliable (produce consistent results) and yet not be valid for use in a given research problem. For example, when intelligence tests are used with subjects from culturally different backgrounds, questions and controversies arise about validity— whether the tests really measure what they purport to measure (intelligence, learning ability)—and not whether they yield consistent scores.

One approach for establishing the validity of measurement uses multiple methods (for example, interviews and observations) of measuring the same and different concepts (Althauser and Heberlein, 1970; Campbell and Fiske, 1959). Studies of the validity of marital and family power have sometimes used the multimethod multitrait matrix approach (Cromwell et al., 1975; Olson and Rabunsky, 1972). Questions about the validity of marriage and family measures could also be raised when they are used in different cultural contexts in which the meaning of the concepts under study are not the same. For example, a marital adjustment or power measure might yield different scores in several cultures because these concepts are regarded differently.

If a measure is valid (assesses what it is supposed to) it must also be reliable (relatively free of random error). No measure can be valid unless it measures the phenomena reliably. On the other hand, instruments that are reliable cannot be used to measure anything. Here we come to a critical point: Measures can be reliable but not valid, but they cannot be valid unless they are reliable. The sections that follow describe more specific conceptions of validity and how it is assessed.

Content Validity

Content validity is concerned with the degree to which a measuring instrument taps the *domain of content* being assessed. If we wanted to measure concept A, represented by the largest circle in Figure 3.1, the content validity issue would be to what degree the measures fully reflect the intended concept. Perhaps the indicators reflect only part of the concept (measures 1 and 2), or perhaps the indicators measure something outside the intended concept (measure 3). In the example

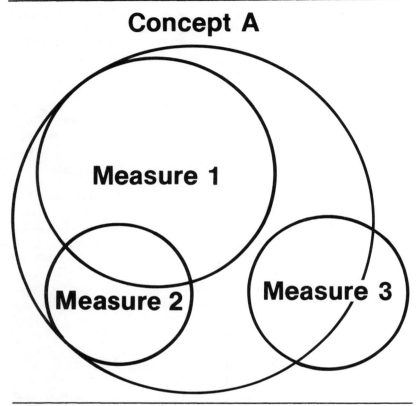

Figure 3.1   Illustration of the Content Validity of Three Measures

shown, measure 1 would be the best measure, because it taps more of the intended concept than the other two measures do. Content validity is simply concerned with the degree to which the indicators tap the domain of content completely and representatively.

Content validity has played a major role in developing instruments when domains of content are particularly clear cut. For example, in developing an arithmetic achievement test, the domain of content would not be adequately covered if addition, subtraction, and division items were included but multiplication items were left out. Unfortunately, most marriage and family concepts are much less clearly defined than arithmetic proficiency. What must be included in measuring the content domain of marital adjustment? Sex-role beliefs? Attachment? Stress?

There are two related problems with content validity for social and behavioral science measures (Carmines and Zeller, 1979: 21-22). The first problem is the difficulty (if not impossibility) of *identifying a generally accepted universe or domain of content* for the concepts to be measured. There simply is not general agreement about what social-behavioral (or marriage and family) concepts should include and exclude. By contrast, there is general agreement that a measure of achievement in basic arithmetic skills must include the four dimensions of addition, subtraction, multiplication, and division. Should a measure of couple or marital adjustment include dimensions of consensus, disagreement, conflict, compatibility, or cohesion (Sharpley and Cross, 1982; Spanier and Thompson, 1982)? Following from the first problem, the second is the *impossibility of randomly sampling* content to create a measure. If the domains of content cannot be agreed upon, it is, of course, not possible to randomly sample items to represent each dimension or domain.

Although the idea of content validity is important, and investigators usually attempt to address it in some way, there is no way of establishing it except by agreement and "appeals to reason" (Nunnally, 1978: 93). Some investigators ask "experts" in the content area to make judgments about the adequacy of the indicators and overall measure, but these attempts are less than compelling evidence for content validity. Even while endorsing the procedures of content validity and their presumptive value, some social scientists have rejected the concept of content validity because there is no rigorous way of assessing it empirically (Bohrnstedt, 1983). As a result of this state of affairs, investigators and critics frequently contend over how well the measures tap the intended concept.

Criterion-Related Validity

If validity, in general, is the degree to which an instrument assesses what it is supposed to, then criterion-related validity is the relationship between the measuring instrument and that external criterion that it is supposed to measure. Criterion-related validity could be assessed, for example, by showing how well an occupational ability test correlates with performance on the job, or how well a partner compatibility test correlates with marital stability or marital adjustment.

Sometimes criterion-related validity is differentiated by whether the criterion is assessed at the same time as the measuring instrument (*concurrent validity*) or at some future time (*predictive validity*). For example, a marital adjustment instrument could be given to distressed couples visiting a clinic and to "normal" couples as a way of demonstrating the *concurrent* validity of the instrument—their scores should be different if the instrument really measures current marital adjustments. *Predictive* validity could be demonstrated by giving the marital adjustment instrument to newly married couples, and on the basis of their scores predicting which marriages would be most likely to end in divorce. In the case of concurrent validation the measuring instrument is correlated with the criterion at approximately the same point in time; with predictive validation the key issue is the degree to which scores on the measuring instrument correspond to a later criterion behavior.

As in the marital compatibility example given, there are clear cases when criterion-related validity would be very important evidence in establishing the value of a test or instrument. For example, premarital relationship instruments such as PREPARE (Fournier et al., 1983) should be able to show predictive validity; that is, they should be substantially correlated with future commitment in marriage, and also with later marital stability. Fowers and Olson (n.d.) recently reported on a study of 148 couples who were studied during their engagement and then followed up three years later. PREPARE scores from the engagement could discriminate between couple relationships that ended in divorce after three years versus those who were happily married.

There are, however, many important marriage and family concepts, as well as more general social and behavioral constructs, for which it is very difficult to assess criterion-related validity.

> While the logic of criterion-related validity is straightforward and its use often compelling in certain practical situations, this type of validity has severe limitations for the social sciences. Most important, for many if not most of the measures used in the social sciences, there simply do not exist any relevant criterion variables. For example, what would be an appropriate criterion variable for a measure of self-esteem? [Zeller and Carmines, 1980: 80].

If there is an area where scores on a measuring instrument have some obvious or logical connection to a particular criterion (like marital adjustment and stability), then assessing criterion-related validity would be both appropriate and desirable. Unlike content validity, criterion-related validity is a rather straightforward empirical matter. The correlation between the measure and the criterion is regarded as the validity coefficient.

Construct Validity

Construct validity is based on theoretical expectations about the way a measure should perform. Evidence for the construct validity of a measure is obtained when theoretically predicted relationships are empirically confirmed. Because of the limitations of both content and criterion-related validity mentioned earlier, it was recognized decades ago that "construct validity must be investigated whenever no criterion or universe of content is accepted as entirely adequate to define the quality to be measured" (Cronbach and Meehl, 1955: 282). Excellent recent treatments of measurement in the social sciences have likewise emphasized that construct validity is preeminently important (Carmines and Zeller, 1979; Zeller and Carmines, 1980, chap. 4).

As an example, suppose that an investigator wanted to be able to say something about the validity of a newly developed measure of sex-role orientation. Suppose the sex-role orientation measure was meant to assess what is regarded as *appropriate* behavior for males and females (not how males and females differ, what they are like, or personal sex-role identity). Unfortunately, there is no clearly agreed upon universe of content from which to choose items for the instrument, although it would be desirable to maximize the content adequacy of the measure. Similarly, there is no logical criterion behavior or characteristic that such a scale should diagnose or predict. But, from theoretical reasoning and literature about sex-role orientations, the investigators (Brogan and Kutner, 1976) predicted that the new measure of sex-role orientation would be related to sex (males being more traditional), educational attainment (those less educated being most traditional), age (older persons being more traditional), religion (Catholics being most traditional), and so on. Their claims that the scale measured what it was supposed to is strengthened by empirically confirming these theoretically predicted relationships. This example should clarify the statement that construct validity is strengthened to the extent that a measure performs in accordance with theoretical expectations.

USING EXISTING MEASURES

Now that some of the complexities of measurement have been explained it should be clear that good measurement is not easily achieved. Most researchers can recount personal experiences to illustrate that what they thought would be an adequate measure turned out not to be. Because developing and refining an instrument is very time consuming, and the quality of an instrument can only be improved over time, using measures that have been previously developed is often a wise decision. Using the same measures also enhances the comparability of research results, making replications, refutations, and accumulating evidence more plausible. Of course, there is no virtue in using a bad instrument just because it is available. It is my opinion, however, that far too often "new" measures are developed carelessly when using previously refined instruments would have made the research stronger. For this reason, the efforts of some social scientists to carefully construct useful instruments should be better known.

Sources of Instruments

Table 3.1 provides an alphabetical listing of measurement inventories that could be useful in assessing marriages and families. Most of these inventories are of general interest to those who would measure human behavior, with those by Buros being the best known and most comprehensive. Others focus directly on marriage and family measurement (especially Olson et al., 1982; Straus and Brown, 1978); assessing children (Johnson and Bommarito, 1971; Walker, 1973), or older adults (Mangen and Peterson, 1982). The book by Straus and Brown (1978) is the most comprehensive and thorough statement about family measurement available.

It must be recognized that existing instruments are not necessarily good measures. In many cases, however, researchers can greatly benefit from long-term instrument development and refinement in selecting or creating their own measures.

TABLE 3.1
Sources of Measuring Instruments

Bonjean, C. M., R. J. Hill, and S. D. McLemore (1967) Sociological Measurement: An Inventory of Scales and Indices. San Francisco: Chandler.

Buros, O. K. (1972). Seventh Mental Measurements Yearbook. Highland Park, NJ: Gryphone Press.

Buros, O. K. (1974) Tests in Print II. Highland Park, NJ: Gryphone Press.

Chun, K., S. Cobb, and R. P. French, Jr. (1975). Measures for Psychological Assessment. Ann Arbor: University of Michigan.

Cromwell, R. E. and D. C. Fournier (forthcoming). Diagnosing Relationships: A Measurement Handbook for Marital and Family Therapists. San Francisco: Jossey-Bass.

Johnson, O. G. and J. W. Bommarito (1971) Tests and Measurements in Child Development: A Handbook. San Francisco: Jossey-Bass.

Lake, D. G., M. B. Miles, and R. B. Earle (1973) Measuring Human Behavior. New York: Teachers College Press.

Mangen, D. J. and W. A. Peterson (1982a) Research Instruments in Social Gerontology: Vol. 1, Clinical and Social Psychology. Minneapolis: University of Minnesota Press.

Mangen, D. J. and W. A. Peterson (1982b) Research Instruments in Social Gerontology. Vol. II, Social Roles and Social Participation. Minneapolis: University of Minnesota Press.

Miller, D. C. (1970) Handbook of Research Design and Social Measurement (2nd ed.). New York: David McKay.

Olson, D. H., H. I. McCubbin, H. Barnes, A. Larsen, M. Muxen, and M. Wilson (1982) Family Inventories. St. Paul: Department of Family Social Science, University of Minnesota.

Robinson, J. P. and P. R. Shaver (1969) Measures of Social Psychological Attitudes. Ann Arbor: University of Michigan Press.

Shaw, M. W. and J. M. Wright (1967) Scales for the Measurement of Attitudes. San Francisco: McGraw-Hill.

Straus, M. A. (1969) Family Measurement Techniques. Minneapolis: University of Minnesota Press.

Straus, M. A. and B. W. Brown (1978) Family Measurement Technique: Abstracts of Published Instruments 1935-1975 (rev. ed.) Minneapolis: University of Minnesota Press.

Walker, D. K. (1973) Socioemotional Measures for Preschool and Kindergarten Children. San Francisco: Jossey-Bass.

SUMMARY

Measurement is the critical link between ideas and reality, between concepts and data. Operational definitions describe the operations necessary to produce scores for the subjects being studied. Measurement must be as systematic and error free as possible for the results to be valid, interpretable, and meaningful.

Some variables can be measured by a single item, but many constructs are best measured with composite indices. This is because multiple indicators combined are likely to provide a more complete and accurate reflection of that which is being studied.

Some variables (like sex or marital status) vary categorically and measurement consists of simply naming each category and perhaps associating a number with it. The nominal level of measurement assesses differences in kind, not in amount or degree. Other levels of measurement are designed to capture continuous variables that range in amount or degree along a continuum. Ordinal measurement means that the property being measured has a "more or less" property; subjects can be ranked in an order on the variable being measured. Interval level of measurement means that the continuous data not only can be ranked, but there are naturally occurring equal distances (or intervals) between points of measurement. The ratio level of measurement is the same as interval-level data except that the scale has an absolute zero.

Two critically important measurement issues are reliability and validity. Reliability is a property of the measurement instrument or procedure itself; it is the degree to which the true score is captured by the measurement. Measures must be reliable for research to be meaningful. Validity is the degree to which the measure reflects the intended construct or taps what is supposed to be measured. Measures must be reliable to be valid.

There are literally hundreds (perhaps thousands) of instruments that have been developed to measure important marriage and family variables. In most cases investigators would be well advised to use, or at least build on, the measurement efforts of their predecessors rather than starting from scratch.

KEY CONCEPTS

Measurement
Operational definition
Item, indicator, indicant
Index, composite score

Scale
Level of measurement
    Nominal
    Ordinal
    Interval
    Ratio
Reliability
    Stability (test-retest, intrarater)
    Equivalence (split half, internal consistency, interrater)
Validity
    Content, face, social
    Criterion related (concurrent, predictive)
    Construct
Existing instruments

CHAPTER

4

Sampling

Every man is in certain respects
Like all other men
Like some other men
Like no other man.

Kluckholm and Murray

SAMPLING HAS TO DO with who (or what) is chosen to be studied. Sometimes researchers want to know about marriages or families with certain characteristics or problems. Other researchers might want to study marriages and families in general; their subjects (marriages, families) would need to be drawn on a broader, perhaps national, basis. In most instances it would be impossible or impractical to actually include all families who could be studied; it would take too long, be too expensive, and reduce the accuracy of the information obtained. For these reasons—efficiency, economy, and accuracy—methods for choosing representative subgroups have been devised by social scientists.

How subgroups are chosen, or sampling, has an important bearing on how the results of research can be interpreted. In many cases the research will be more valuable if those being studied are selected through a precise and deliberate strategy. Sometimes, however, a very carefully controlled sampling plan is not so important. How the sample should be selected depends upon the purposes of the research. A quick, preliminary exploration of a marriage or family issue, or the study of a low-frequency event, or an accurate estimate of marital or family behaviors on which public policies might be based would each call for different sampling strategies.

Systematic advances in sampling procedures have occurred most rapidly in social science disciplines such as political science and sociology. Perhaps this is because these disciplines make frequent use of large-scale surveys of the general population. Marriage and family scholars have borrowed much from the sampling procedures of these base disciplines, and only recently has attention been focused on the state of sampling in marriage and family research per se (Kitson et al., 1982).

DEFINITIONS

In general use the term *sample* means a subset or part of the whole. A cook might sample a soup by sipping just a spoonful, and a family researcher's sample might consist of a relatively small number of all those he or she is trying to investigate. In more scientific terms, a sample is the group or subset of cases that is selected from the total population to be studied. Each one of the cases (individuals, marriages, or families) chosen to be studied is called a *sample element*. In other words, the group of sample elements chosen to be studied make up the sample that is part of a larger population. Sometimes the group of subjects actually studied is referred to as the sample, regardless of whether or not this group was deliberately selected from some previously identified population. The concept of a sample, though, has its clearest meaning in relationship to the population. The *population* is the group to which one would like to be able to generalize the results after studying the sample.

In order to be able to generalize sample findings to the population it is critically important that the sample not be *biased*, or systematically different than the population. After studying marital decision-making processes among young married couples, for example, it would not be appropriate to generalize the results to middle-aged couples or to couples in general. The key issue in generalizing from a sample to a population is representativeness: The sample must represent, or be like, the population. A *representative sample* is the opposite of a sample that is biased; a sample is representative if its characteristics are distributed in every important way as they are in the population.

APPROACHES TO SAMPLING

Following generally accepted conventions in the social sciences, and a more focused discussion of sampling in family studies per se (Kitson et al., 1982), samples can be grouped into two major categories. *Probability samples* are drawn from a known population in such a way that it is possible to calculate the likelihood (hence the name "probability") of each case being included in the sample. Probability samples also make it possible to estimate the margin of error between the sample data and what would be found if the entire population were studied (Sudman, 1976). *Nonprobability samples* are all of the rest—groups of subjects from populations that are not defined and in which it is impossible to estimate potential biases introduced by the sampling method. In spite of the greater precision and exactness of probability samples, nonprobability samples have an important place in marriage and family research.

Nonprobability Samples

Nonprobability samples are the only choice in certain research situations and they are probably the better choice in others. If the population cannot be clearly identified, then a nonprobability approach must be taken. For example, a doctoral student once wanted to do an exploratory study of bisexuals (persons without predominately heterosexual or homosexual preferences). Because such individuals are relatively rare and are not from any known, identifiable population, the student had no choice but to study the small number of bisexuals whom he could find and interview. Although he could and did describe the subjects in his study, it is impossible to determine if those whom he interviewed were like bisexuals in general; he could not really generalize his conclusions about the characteristics of bisexuals beyond the small group he had studied.

Even if a representative sample of an identifiable population could be drawn, it might not be the most practical approach if the phenomenon being studied occurs rarely among the sample elements. Zelnik and colleagues did draw a probability sample to study adolescent pregnancy between the ages of 15 and 19, but they were concerned about the inefficiency of this approach because they wanted to focus on those adolescents who were or had been pregnant (Zelnik et al., 1981). In the case of adolescent pregnancy, a large number of interviews were wasted in the probability sample of teenagers because many had not experienced the phenomenon of interest.

Nonprobability samples are, in general, most appropriate when the researcher wants to study subjects from a population that has not been, or cannot be, defined. These studies often are more exploratory and qualitative, hypothesis generating rather than hypothesis testing. Nonprobability samples are also more feasible if the focus of the research is on a relatively low-frequency event (such as group marriage or childlessness) that would appear so infrequently in a broader survey that the costs required to capture an adequate sample would be prohibitive.

Nonprobability samples are known by many names. An *accidental* or *convenience* sample is well described by its name; subjects are included because they are "convenient" and, usually, near at hand. Subjects in convenience samples are often recruited from classes or other groups, or they might volunteer in response to advertisements or announcements.

Snowball sampling is another nonprobability technique that is most likely to be used when it is particularly difficult to identify potential subjects. Snowball sampling begins with a small number of subjects who refer others they know to the investigator; these others who become subjects refer still others, and so on, like the analogy of a snowball gaining size as it rolls downhill. In the study of bisexuals previously mentioned, subjects were identified through a snowball sampling technique. Using a network of subjects known to and referred by others has both advantages and limitations. It might be the only way possible to identify subjects who are hard to locate, and those who are part of a cohesive network might be more committed to participation in the study. There is a serious risk, however, that the sample will be biased to an unknowable extent because individuals who are not part of the social network will not be referred to the researcher and included in the sample.

Quota sampling was developed as an expedient way of obtaining public opinion data, and it has been refined to become the basis of highly accurate contemporary political polls. A quota sample is selected by setting quotas for including subjects with specific characteristics, such as sex, age, and race. These quotas are set to approximate the distribution of known salient characteristics in the general population. Using known population characteristics and an increased understanding of key variables, pollsters have made considerable practical use of quota sampling. Quota samples have rarely been used by marriage and family researchers.

A *purposive* sample consists of subjects chosen because they are thought by the researcher to be representative of the larger population being studied. Subjects are selected "purposively" because of their characteristics. In the 1970s a great deal of interest was being expressed about formalizing theory and theory construction tools in studies of marriage and the family. To assess the interests and activities of family theorists, Klein et al. (1977) sent a survey to family professionals who were purposively chosen because they had attended theory workshops or published theoretical articles or books. There is no way of knowing how well the results obtained from a purposive sample actually characterize or represent some larger population of interest.

Probability Samples

A *simple random sample* is obtained if the procedures followed allow each sample element an equal opportunity to be selected. In actual practice such samples are rarely used because the sample elements (households, families, or subjects) must all be listed, numbered, and selected by a random procedure one case at a time. Because this is such a tedious process if the population is large, several short cuts have been devised.

A *systematic random sample*, like the simple random sample, requires a complete listing of population elements. However, after the sampling fraction (the number of elements to be included in the sample divided by the number in the population) is decided upon, the systematic procedure is to select only the first sample element randomly. After the first random selection from the population, every Nth case (the width of the sample interval) is automatically included in the sample. Each case has a chance of being included in a systematic random sample because the first choice is made randomly. The practical advantage of the systematic sample over the simple random sample is apparent; the random selection only has to be made once rather than for each sample element. This saves time and effort because thereafter every Nth case is included in the sample instead of having to go back and forth between the new random number and the listing of all sample elements.

Stratified sampling is done to increase the probability that the sample will represent accurately the population being studied. The sample is stratified only on variables that are thought, or are known, to be related to the focus of the study. If, for example, a sample is being drawn to study attitudes about gender roles, it would be very important to try and maximize the representativeness of the responses of both men and women. In the past, women have been more accessible to survey workers and in a simple random sample more women than men are likely to complete interviews. Employed women, however, might be least likely to participate, and employment probably has an important association with women's gender-role attitudes. It might make sense in such a study to first stratify the population by sex and employment status, and then to draw random samples from each group or strata. The sample might be a *proportionate* stratified random sample if cases are selected proportional to their numbers in the population, or a *disproportionate* stratified sample selected because the numbers in the general population are so small that a proportional sample would mean a high risk of sampling error because of the few cases chosen.

When studying very large populations neither simple nor systematic random samples are very feasible because of the requirement that all sample elements need to be listed and uniquely identified. In addition, if direct interviews were being used to collect the data, it would be very expensive to send interviewers to hundreds (or thousands) of spread-out locations. *Cluster, area,* or *multistage* sampling is used to draw probability samples of large populations. These procedures begin by first sampling from among large geographic areas (or clusters) such as states, regions, or large metropolitan areas. Within each of the areas chosen, samples are drawn of smaller geographic units (such as census tracts). Then samples are drawn of neighborhoods and eventually households and families. An example that contains a large amount of marriage and family data is the study on the quality of American life conducted by Campbell and associates in 1976. As the term *multistage sample* suggests, these procedures proceed from all-inclusive large areas to smaller, less inclusive sampling units until households and the actual respondents are eventually identified.

SUMMARY

A sample or subset of the population is that group of subjects chosen to be studied. Sampling is done for efficiency, economy, and accuracy. Sample elements can be chosen with a very precise probability sampling technique so that the likelihood of selection is known or can be calculated. Approaches to probability sampling include simple random, systematic random, stratified random, and area, cluster, or multistage sampling.

Nonprobability samples are chosen from an unknown population and consequently the probability of a sample element being selected cannot be determined. Approaches to nonprobability sampling include convenience or accidental, snowball, quota, and purposive sampling.

If one wants to be able to generalize results obtained with the sample to the larger population (as is often the case), the key issue is representativeness. If the sample is not biased but is representative (like the population in every respect), sample findings can be generalized to the population.

KEY CONCEPTS

Sample
Population
Sample element
Biased sample
Representative sample
Sampling frame
Sampling interval
Nonprobability sample
    Convenience, accidental sample
    Snowball sample

       Quota sample
       Purposive sample
   Probability sample
       Simple random sample
       Systematic random sample
       Stratified random sample
       Cluster, area, multistage sample
   Generalizability

CHAPTER

5

Data Collection

Observe, probe
Details unfold.
Let nature's secrets
Be stammeringly retold.

Goethe

EACH OF THE PRECEDING CHAPTERS has been about preliminary steps that are usually taken before data are gathered systematically. It would not make much sense to collect data until having a pretty clear idea of what you were trying to find out and how you were going to go about it. Based on some idea, insight, or theoretical expectation, research questions or objectives must first be formulated to guide the research. The research questions, objectives, or hypotheses have important implications for how the study will be designed, how key variables will be measured, and how a sample will be chosen to be studied. Once the conceptual, design, measurement, and sampling decisions have been made, data collection is the next logical step in the research process.

In any given study the steps prior to collecting data might have consisted primarily of thinking about and discussing ideas and making preparations. In collecting data, however, researchers usually leave the sanctuaries of their minds, offices, and libraries to confront practical matters in the real world. Data collection might consist of actually getting out into the field to interview or observe people, or it might involve bringing them into a lab for more controlled observations, or going through files, microfilms, or tapes of public records at a courthouse or some other data repository. In contrast to preliminary research activities that are largely mental, data collection is a physically active "get-your-hands-dirty" stage in conducting a study.

In anticipation of collecting data the researcher must make preparations so that usable information will be acquired as systematically and smoothly as possible. Some of the important tasks to be accomplished are gaining access to the sample, obtaining their cooperation and consent, pretesting the instruments, and preparing to actually acquire the best data possible.

GAINING COOPERATION

Sometimes the data to be collected are part of the public domain and gaining cooperation is either a moot issue or a rather minor one. For example, observations of couples with and without children in public places (Rosenblatt, 1974) can be done without anyone's permission. And, it might be rather routine to fill out some forms or talk to a public official in order to take data from public records such as divorce court files.

Having three young children, I have often thought about systematically observing parent-child interaction in grocery stores, especially around the checkout counter. (You might have noticed that these gatelike spaces that customers and their children must pass through are packed with rows of candy.) It is not likely that the manager would let me or my observers stand around with our clipboards or tape recorders very long, however, unless we had obtained permission. In arranging access for this grocery store observation, it would probably even be better if the manager would allow observers to record parent-child behaviors from the booth or office they use to watch for shoplifters. This request, however, begins to encroach on the space, time, and regular routines of the store's operation. This brings us to some central issues in gaining access: why do some people cooperate with researchers whereas others refuse to participate?

In one study, our research team had been contracted to do a survey of family relationships and the sexual attitudes and behaviors of high school students. After months of planning we had clearly in mind what we wanted to do and how we could do it most efficiently. We prepared our surveys and drew a random sample (stratified by school size) of 12 high schools in our state. Over his signature, the state superintendent of public schools sent out the letter we had written explaining the research to district administrators over the 12 schools, and asked for their cooperation. Because the State Office of Education was our sponsor and the state superintendent was endorsing our project, we expected little difficulty in gaining access to the 12 schools and their students. We could not have been more wrong. Regardless of who endorsed or sponsored the research, 4 of the 12 district superintendents "politely declined" to allow a study of sexual attitudes and behavior to be conducted at their schools. Rather than severely compromising our random sample of schools, we decided to change our data collection procedures. Instead of sampling students from official school records and interviewing them at school, we devised what turned out to be a better plan. At all 12 schools we obtained the widely distributed student directory listing student names, addresses, and phone numbers. We drew our random sample of students from these directories. Next, we mailed a letter of introduction and then telephoned the parents of students directly. After we obtained both parent and student permission, we completed interviews at home with about three-quarters of all students who had been sampled.

We had not anticipated that upper-level administrators would deny access to schools, but they were extremely uncomfortable with such sensitive questions being asked at school. They were, or perceived themselves to be, at risk. As it turned out, parents were more willing to give consent than were the administrators, and the privacy at home made the interviews better than if they would have been conducted at school.

Sometimes access or entry must be allowed by school administrators, business managers, agency officials, parents, or some other gatekeepers before family researchers can even approach the subjects about participating. Even then, unless the research is part of the public domain or subjects are young children, subjects themselves must cooperate for data to be collected. Both gatekeepers and subjects have several reasons for being reluctant to cooperate with requests to conduct research. It is almost certain to take some of their valuable time

TABLE 5.1
Obstacles in Obtaining Cooperation and
Some Possible Solutions for Overcoming Them

Obstacles	*Possible Solutions*
It takes my time.	Offer incentives such as information, money, goods, or services.
I'm not interested.	Appeal to altruism (every response is crucial, helping advance science); offer incentives.
It would cost me money.	Pay all expenses in advance.
It interrupts established routines.	Minimize interruptions and staff worker involvement.
It's invasive, too personal.	Assure confidentiality or anonymity.
I'd be at risk.	Assure confidentiality or anonymity; show benefits.

and interrupt their usual routines. For subjects, especially in the case of marriage and family research, the research questions might be uncomfortably personal, invasive, or risky. How do researchers gain cooperation to study marital conflict, or ask about marital intimacies or extramarital affairs, for example?

It is more difficult to obtain the cooperation of subjects and public officials for some studies than others. This difficulty of obtaining cooperation may come from the sensitive nature of the topic under investigation, or from the personal reluctance, fears, or uncertainties of the persons involved. Because obtaining cooperation can make or break a study, Table 5.1 shows a number of obstacles to obtaining cooperation and some possible ways of overcoming them.

PROTECTING HUMAN SUBJECTS

The preceding discussion about gaining the cooperation of gate-keepers and subjects raises the fundamental ethical issue of *informed consent*. Informed consent means that enough information about the study is given to individuals so that they can make an informed choice about whether or not to participate. Informed consent regulations originally came about to prevent medical and biological research abuses, such as giving untested drugs to people who were not informed or who had not given consent, and experimenting with subjects in vulnerable populations (welfare recipients, prisoners, mental patients) who might feel compelled to participate. The blanket federal regulations, however, have been applied to all research involving human subjects. The major elements of informed consent include: (1) an explanation of the study's purposes and procedures; (2) a description of potential risks; (3) a description of potential benefits; (4) disclosure of alternative procedures that might benefit subjects; (5) an offer to answer any questions; and (6) an assurance that subjects are free to withdraw from the research at any time for any reason.

Informed consent regulations have undoubtedly helped to protect the rights of human subjects in research, and to heighten the awareness of social science researchers to possible ethical problems in their procedures (American Psychological Association, 1973; American Sociological Association, 1969). But they have also created some difficult problems for social scientists (Diener and Crandall, 1978; Reynolds, 1979) and for marriage and family researchers in particular (LaRossa et al., 1981). Because the human subjects regulations were developed primarily to protect subjects from physical harm, they have sometimes been difficult, if not impossible, to apply to field research (Duster et al., 1979). This is of particular concern because telling subjects what is being studied and what is expected often will distort their responses and make the study worthless. On the other hand, subjects have the right not to be tricked or deceived into doing things that could be potentially harmful to them (Thompson, 1981).

The problem of informed consent becomes even more acute for qualitative family researchers because they make a deliberate attempt to remain flexible in order to pursue ideas and insights that emerge unexpectedly. In short, the qualitative investigator approaches data collection not knowing all that will transpire, issues are often very personal, and other persons and activities might be unexpectedly discussed by the subject during an interview session. "Thus, more than any other investigators, a qualitative family researcher cannot know, nor can he or she explain to the subjects at the outset, just who or what will be examined as part of the research" (LaRossa et al., 1981: 305).

A large amount of marriage and family research involves children, and their participation raises additional issues about informed consent. Children might be more vulnerable to stress, have less knowledge and experience, and are less able to evaluate what their participation in research might mean. There are specific regulations governing research on children (U.S. Department of Health and Human Services, 1983), but basically the legal requirement is that researchers must obtain the informed written consent of parents for their minor children to be involved in research. Depending on their age and understanding, children also need to be informed and asked to give their consent, and children's rights are considered always to supersede the rights of investigators (Society for Research in Child Development, 1973).

In summary, collecting data requires at least an ethical consideration and respect for the rights of human subjects. Government regulations require any research supported by federal funds to be reviewed by an Institutional Review Board (IRB) to safeguard the rights of human subjects. A key element of subjects' rights, especially in regard to data collection, is their informed consent. As some family researchers have written: "We see the major problem as one of balancing the need to penetrate the private, pervasive and emotional back regions of family life against the tempting, and often easy, violation of a family's privacy and hospitality" (LaRossa et al., 1981: 312).

PILOT STUDIES AND PRETESTS

To be comparable across all subjects, data need to be collected as systematically or uniformly as possible. In the real world of data collection, however, many things can go wrong. It is probably a rarity for data to be gathered without some major or minor problem arising. Poor data collection procedures are a common source of error in the data, and inconsistent procedures can become a serious threat to, or even completely destroy, a study. A large amount of data can become of questionable value or rendered useless if a serious problem in procedures is discovered part way through the study.

One way of avoiding—or at least reducing—the many logistical difficulties of data collection is to do a pilot study or pretest. A *pilot study* is a mini-study done in advance of a larger, more complex and expensive research project. A pilot study is conducted in just the same way as the larger study has been planned so that all of the research procedures, instruments, and even preliminary analyses are tried out. The pilot study helps to identify possible problems and sort the "bugs" out so that time, energy, and money will not be wasted in the larger study to follow. An appropriate analogy for seafarers might be the "shake-down cruise" a ship takes before being committed to a longer stay at sea.

In a sloppy sort of way a pilot study might be referred to as a pretest, but the term pretest has two very specific research meanings. As already explained in Chapter 2, a pretest is sometimes given before a treatment and an identical posttest in an experimental or quasi-experimental design. Considered in the present context, though, along with a pilot study, a *pretest* means that the measuring instrument to be used is pretested or tried out in advance of actual data collection. It is sound research practice to pretest instruments with subjects like those who will participate in the actual study. The purpose of the pretest in this context is not actually to collect data, but to refine, sharpen, and de-bug instruments *before* data collection begins. Unclear coding categories for observer ratings or ambiguous or inappropriate language in survey protocols can be detected by trying the instruments out before data are collected.

MODES OF DATA COLLECTION

Some modes of data collection are rather *obtrusive* because they intrude on the subjects' awareness and perhaps even change the attitudes or behaviors being studied. On the other hand, it is sometimes possible to collect data surreptitiously or *unobtrusively* so that subjects do not even know they are being studied (for example, our hypothetical grocery store observation of parents and children). In a classic statement (Webb et al., 1966) and restatement (Webb et al., 1981) about unobtrusive measurement, a persuasive argument was made about the weaknesses of relying only on interviews and questionnaires. These survey tools "intrude as a foreign element into the social setting they would describe, they create as well as measure attitudes, they elicit atypical roles and responses, and they are limited to those who are accessible and will cooperate" (Webb et al., 1981: 1). The authors called for supplementing the use of surveys, to which respondents react, with unobtrusive or nonreactive measures that tap the same variables but that have different methodological weaknesses.

Some procedures are quite *direct*, such as counting the frequency of a target behavior (e.g., parent saying "no"), whereas other procedures might be much more *indirect*, such as inferring relationship qualities from a written response. Some modes of data collection rely on the respondents' or *insiders'* self-report of their own perceptions, whereas other modes rely on the external assessment of *outsiders* (Olson, 1977).

Although there are many methods of collecting data, this chapter will be selective and focus on those of greatest importance to marriage and family researchers. Family researchers have used surveys more than any other method (Hodgson and Lewis, 1979), whereas developmental psychologists have tended to rely on direct observations (Brody and Endsley, 1981; Furstenberg, 1985). Although historical (Elder, 1981; Laslett, 1972; Wrigley and Schofield, 1981) and demographic (Blake, 1981; Teachman, 1983) procedures appear to be increasingly common in family studies, the focus here will be on surveys and observations.

Survey Data Collection

All surveys rely on self-reports; they consist of asking people questions. If the research topic is one that respondents could and would tell you about or, perhaps, something that only they know about, a survey approach is clearly warranted. Sometimes surveys focus solely on marriage, or kinship, or parenting, and so on. Even in much broader social science surveys, however, and even in the census, many key marriage and familial variables—such as marital status, length of marriage, number of children, and so on—are usually included. As a result, there is a wealth of survey data about marriages and families.

There are several approaches to collecting survey data; these are: (1) questionnaires, (2) direct (face-to-face) interviews, and (3) telephone interviews. Although each of these techniques is currently used in marriage and family surveys, telephone interviews have really only come into use since about 1980. The strategies, strengths, and limitations of each approach will be considered in turn below.

Questionnaires. Surveys in which respondents mark their own answers are called questionnaires. They have been used extensively in marriage and family research, probably because they are relatively simple, fast, and inexpensive. Questionnaires are usually mailed to respondents or administered in a group setting such as a classroom. There literally have been thousands of college classes in which students have been surveyed about their families of orientation, dating and courtship experiences, their sexual attitudes, and various other marriage and family topics.

In addition to being fast and economical, questionnaires can be administered so that respondents remain anonymous. *Anonymity* means that the respondent *cannot* be identified. If there are no identifying marks or numbers on the questionnaire and respondents are told that they cannot be traced, it is likely that responses will be more complete. Although mailed questionnaires must be sent to specific addresses and they are usually coded to permit followup contacts in the case of nonresponse, they could be returned anonymously, without any identifiers at all. More commonly, however, anonymous questionnaires are administered in a group and passed back in so that respondents cannot be identified (much like teacher evaluations). Guaranteeing anonymity might be an important advantage in encouraging complete responses, particularly when what is being studied is socially sensitive (premarital sex, homosexuality) or illegal (drug use, criminal behavior).

The questionnaire is a relatively fast and inexpensive way of collecting data because interviewers do not need to be recruited, trained, and sent out to obtain the responses. Questionnaires thus greatly reduce the personnel costs that are a necessary part of interviewing. Researchers using mailed questionnaire surveys have developed a rather specialized methodology in recent years (see Dillman, 1978, for example). These efforts have been successful at maximizing the response rate to mailed surveys (Goyder, 1982; Heberlein and Baumgartner, 1978).

Because of the advantages mentioned above, questionnaires have been used widely, perhaps even when another strategy of data collection would have been more appropriate. Questionnaires do not allow the checks on data quality that interviews do. For example, if respondents to a mailed survey do not understand a written question, it cannot be clarified. If the respondent's answer is incomplete or inappropriate, there is no way to probe further for a more adequate response. If some questions are contingent on previous answers, or if there are other complexities, the questionnaire respondent is likely to become frustrated or confused. In other words, the questionnaire is only useful with respondents who are literate, and it is most useful with those who are better educated. In addition, questions and the survey format need to be as simple and straightforward as possible to avoid confusion.

Questionnaires, then, are best suited to somewhat simple rather than deep or complex research issues. Although it would be an overstatement to say categorically that questionnaires are quick and dirty, they are fast and there are legitimate concerns about data quality.

Direct (face-to-face) interviews. The key difference between a questionnaire and interview is the interviewer. *Interviews* are surveys in which an interviewer asks the questions and records the responses. Face-to-face interviews conducted by trained personnel have been the preferred method of data collection at most large survey research centers. Schuman (1982: 27) has observed that large-scale sample surveys in the early years regularly succeeded in completing interviews with 80% to 85% of those sampled, but "in the last 20 years, this figure has declined until even 75 percent is considered relatively good, and 65 percent is by no means uncommon." Although direct interviews are much more expensive than questionnaires, they provide greater flexibility, can achieve much greater depth and complexity, and result in more complete and accurate data. These are critically important advantages to be considered against their high cost.

In marriage and family research there are several situations in which face-to-face interviews would be the clearly preferred method of data collection. As suggested above, one of these would be when the investigator wanted to probe deeply into the subtleties and complexities of an issue. Face-to-face interviews would also be the method of choice if the investigator wasn't quite sure exactly what questions should be asked in a structured questionnaire; in this case the interviewer would proceed in a semi-structured way by raising topics and issues rather than asking standardized questions to be answered with fixed alternatives (LaRossa and LaRossa, 1981; Gelles, 1974).

If necessary, interviewers can clarify questions, probe for greater detail or specificity, elicit continued cooperation when objections are raised or interest lags, and so on. Professional survey centers go to great lengths to train interviewers and evaluate their performance because they make the critical difference in data quality (Institute for Social Research, 1976; Thornton et al., 1982).

Telephone interviews. In a very real sense telephone interviews have emerged as a practical alternative choice between the high quality but expensive face-to-face interview, and the quick, inexpensive, but more superficial questionnaire. Telephone interviews combine the advantages of remarkable speed and relative economy with interviewer monitoring and respondent interaction. The result is relatively inexpensive, high-quality data. Studies comparing response rates and data quality of telephone and face-to-face interviews generally show telephone surveys to be virtually equal in both (Jordan et al., 1980).

Although phone surveys generally are found to be somewhat more likely to be terminated, this could depend a great deal on the topic or content of the interviews.

This data collection technique has become more feasible to use in studies of the general population as telephones have come to be found in nearly every household. As phones have become more widely distributed, however, unlisted telephone numbers have also increased. The technical solution to this problem is random digit dialing, so that every household with a telephone has a chance of being included as part of the sample, regardless of whether it has a listed or unlisted telephone number (Klecka and Tuchfarber, 1978).

Very few marriage and family researchers have used telephone surveys in their work, but this is likely to change as its advantages become more widely understood. One longitudinal study (Huston et al., 1985) of early relationship development used telephone surveys at frequent intervals to keep track of changes in young couples over time. In another recent work (Gelles, 1984), telephone surveys of a national sample provided the data necessary to estimate the incidence of child snatching in the United States. In a telephone study of pets in the family, it has been reported that respondents remain very interested and are willing to talk at great length about their pet(s) (Albert, 1985, personal communication).

In summary, each mode of survey data collection has its advantages and limitations for studying marriages and families. These are displayed in Table 5.2. Refinements in survey methodology are likely to influence how future surveys are carried out. Recently, for example, interesting advances have occurred regarding factors affecting response rates to mailed questionnaires (Dillman, 1978; Heberlein and Baumgartner,

TABLE 5.2
Modes of Survey Data Collection

Mode	Advantages	Disadvantages
Questionnaire	least expensive; fast; can be anonymous	cannot clarify, answer questions, or probe further
Face-to-face interview	validity checks (nonverbal cues); can be very complex; detailed; flexible	most expensive; requires interviewer selection, training, quality control
Telephone interview	very fast; can be anonymous	limited length

1978), the use of open- and closed-question formats (Schuman and Presser, 1979), and the effects of wording on responses obtained (Schuman and Presser, 1981). Perhaps the most significant changes in conducting marriage and family survey research will come about as a result of methodological studies examining the differences in responses through telephone versus face-to-face interviews (Groves and Kahn, 1979). Telephone interviews are substantially faster and about one-fourth the cost of face-to-face data collection (Klecka and Tuchfarber, 1978).

Collecting Data by Observation

In many research situations better data can be acquired by watching subjects than by asking them questions. Infants and young children must be observed rather than surveyed. Some behavioral interaction is so complex that it is best understood by careful observation. If the research goal is to know the frequency of some observable behavior (smiling, touching), an actual count would be better than a self-report. When subjects do not know the answers to questions you might pose, or if they are unlikely to tell the truth ("How often do you 'put down' your spouse in normal conversation?"), observations are more appropriate than self-reports.

Observational methods are systematic procedures for watching behavior and recording what takes place. Observations range from rather general, inclusive, or *molar* approaches to extremely detailed *molecular* analyses of specific behavioral elements. One study, as an example of a very molar observation approach, involved rating each college coed as she returned her questionnaire to the instructor. The researchers had collected most of their data by having respondents fill out a questionnaire. However, a rating of physical attractiveness was obtained by watching each coed as she walked up the front of the class; her attractiveness score was given by placing the questionnaire into one of seven piles according to her "observed" physical attractiveness (Kaats and Davis, 1970). The most attractive coeds described themselves as having been more pressured to engage in sexual relations and to have become more sexually involved. This is an example of a very molar *rating scale* kind of observation in which all of the observed characteristics or behavior are reduced to a single score. More molecular approaches to marriage and family observations are generally of two kinds (Filsinger and Lewis, 1981; Gottman, 1979; Lamb et al.,

1979). The first is called *event sampling* and it consists of counting the frequency of occurrence of specific *target behaviors*. Of all the behaviors that occur during a 20- or 30-minute observation, it might be that researchers are interested only in children's sharing behaviors, or in parents' praising and encouraging their children. Such target behaviors must be defined clearly enough so that observers can code their occurrence reliably.

The second and even more molecular approach to observation is called an *interval* or *time sampling* technique. It has been developed so that observations are divided into very small units, usually 10 seconds or so. At the end of each interval observers record the behaviors that occurred. Again, each behavior to be coded must be carefully defined for observers, but the short intervals make rater agreement easier to obtain. Sometimes time sampling observations are broken into intervals that include alternating segments for watching, recording, watching, recording, and so on. In other cases the continuous or ongoing *stream of behavior* is coded as fully as possible by recording quickly at the end of the timed interval and then immediately beginning the next interval. Even more technically sophisticated *stream of behavior* coding systems use electronic coding devices or videotaping so that all behaviors can be captured and stored for later retrieval and analysis.

There are many important subissues in the observational study of marriages and families. Will the observation take place in a "natural environment" such as the home or a public place (Kantor and Lehr, 1975; Steinglass, 1980), or in an "artificial setting" like a laboratory of some kind (Reiss, 1981)? Closely related, will obtrusive or unobtrusive observation be used? The subject's awareness of being observed raises the issue of reactivity as a concern. For example, in one observation (Miller and Bowen, 1982) of early father-infant interaction in the mother's hospital room, the reactivity of one father to direct observation was obvious; when the nurse-observer entered the room he stopped holding and playing with the baby, returned it to his wife's arms, and turned to watch the television.

Many procedures have been developed for the observational or behavioral assessment of social interaction in general (Lamb et al., 1979) and for assessing marriages (Filsinger and Lewis, 1981) and families (Riskin and Faunce, 1970, 1972) in particular. Some of these consist of categories for scoring interactive behavioral data, whereas others are techniques for stimulating or intensifying routine interaction between family members.

Interaction Process Analysis, or IPA (Bales, 1950), was an important forerunner of coding systems designed especially for marriage and family study. Although the 12 category IPA coding scheme was developed by social psychologists from studies of small ad hoc group interaction, it was used in several early observational studies of couple decision making. It was found that spouses who talked the most during observation had more influence in marital decision making. When these studies first began, wives were clearly more likely than husbands to display a high frequency of affective or socioemotional behaviors (Kenkel and Hoffman, 1956; Strodtbeck, 1950, 1951). Early small group observations of ad hoc and family groups identified the task or instrumental role and the socioemotional role as being the two major positions in small group behavior. This discovery led to a classic (over)statement about the nature of role differentiation in marriage and the family (Parsons and Bales, 1955).

Other researchers have devised various situations and games to stimulate marriage or family interaction so that variables of interest could more readily be observed. The observational study of whole families has been of particular interest to researchers associated with various approaches to marital and family therapy (Reiss, 1981; Riskin and Faunce, 1971; Winter and Ferreira, 1969). Simulated Family Activity measurement (SIMFAM) and Simulation of Career Patterns (SIMCAR) were devised to enable researchers to manipulate variables experimentally and to observe directly various aspects of family behavior and interaction (Straus and Tallman, 1971; Tallman et al., 1974). Another approach has been based on the "revealed difference technique" first described by Strodtbeck (1951) in which couples are confronted with issues about which they have previously given different (conflicting) answers to the investigator. This technique for couple interaction was used in the Color Matching procedure (Goodrich and Boomer, 1963) and later in the Inventory of Marital Conflict (Olson and Ryder, 1970).

SUMMARY

Data collection is the manual labor part of the research process. Research questions cannot be answered, and theoretically expected relationships cannot be detected, unless high-quality data are obtained.

Pretesting instruments and procedures, or conducting a complete pilot study, is an important way of assuring that data collection will be as smooth and problem free as possible.

Obtaining permission to collect data and maintaining cooperation are frequently delicate necessities in marriage and family research. The rights and dignity of human subjects must be protected; they are safeguarded by federal regulations. In most cases subjects must consent to participate after being informed about the research purposes and about the steps that will be taken to protect their identity and minimize risks to them. It is, however, sometimes impossible to fully inform subjects because issues and topics can arise unexpectedly, especially in relatively unstructured field interviews. In other cases, fully informing subjects about research purposes would invalidate the study because of reactivity—subjects would change their responses or behavior to make themselves look better or to help the investigator find what he or she is looking for.

There are many modes and techniques of marriage and family data collection, ranging from taking existing information from records, documents, and archives to asking people questions and observing their behavior. Survey responses collected through questionnaires, personal interviews, and telephone interviews are the most common kind of marriage and family data. Live and recorded observations are also an important source of marriage and family data, especially for the study of processes, interaction, and subjects who will not or can not (infants and young children) verbalize responses to the investigator's questions. An appropriate mode or modes of data collection depend on the research question(s) as well as the practical realities of money, time, and cooperation.

KEY CONCEPTS

Gaining access
Obtaining cooperation
Obstacles to cooperation
Solutions for noncooperation
Protection of human subjects
    Informed consent
    Benefits/risks
    Right to have questions answered
    Right to withdraw
Pilot study

Pretest
Modes of data collection
Existing records and documents
Surveys
    Questionnaire
    Face-to-face interview
    Telephone interview
Observations
    Molar
    Molecular
    Event sampling
    Time or interval sampling
    Stream of behavior
Data quality

CHAPTER

6

Data Analysis

The only thing a computer thinks is that you know what you're doing.
                                                                  Jane Post

IT IS EASY to become lost in data. Data analysis is the process of organizing and arranging data so that the results of the study can be interpreted. By the time that the last interview has been completed, the last questionnaire has been returned, the last observation has been recorded, or the last figures have been obtained, the investigator must know what to do with the data. Ideally, even before data are collected, analysis plans will have been laid out to fit the research questions that guided the study. Specific data analysis plans are usually required, for example, in graduate student thesis proposals or in research proposals submitted to public or private sponsors. However, it is not uncommon to witness or be part of data analysis fishing expeditions or mindless data dredging. The point is, however, that data analysis is most efficient when conducted according to a plan, much like mining is most productive when the miner knows what to look for and where it is most likely to be found.

The specific steps that are followed in analyzing data depend on the kind of data and the type of question(s) being asked. Qualitative data analysis, based on in-depth interviews, might consist solely or mostly of the investigator studying notes or transcripts, classifying occurrences and subjects, and relating examples of general themes or types. Some of the most widely recognized "classic" marriage and family studies have been analyzed in this way (Cuber and Haroff, 1965), as well as more recent studies (Gelles, 1974; LaRossa and LaRossa, 1981).

However, the vast majority of contemporary marriage and family research depends on computer technology and statistical procedures for quantitative data analyses. This is immediately evident from examining any professional journal in which marriage and family research is published. Consequently, this chapter emphasizes quantitative data analysis. Common steps in this form of data analysis include data preparation, data entry, data transformations, and statistical analyses.

DATA PREPARATION AND ENTRY

After being collected, data frequently need to be "prepared" before being entered into a computer. This is usually because the format of data collection (for example, the survey booklet or observers' rating sheet) was not designed so that data could be transferred directly into the computer. For example, verbal answers or observational categories are usually "coded" as numerals that the computer can process more efficiently. Although respondents might have been asked to write out their job title and what they do, their responses would usually be made into an occupational status variable coded in the following way: 1— professionals (doctors, attorneys, etc.), 2—managers, 3—technicians, and so on. Similarly, tally marks on observation sheets might need to be coded so that each one becomes a number that stands for a specific behavior, a behavioral sequence, or the duration of an act.

In some studies the coding of raw data can be extremely time consuming. And, of course, the more complex or tedious the coding, the more likely it is that mistakes will be made. Because coding is time consuming, expensive, and a source of error in the data, technologies have been developed to minimize data preparation requirements. In marriage and family surveys, for example, responses are frequently "precoded" so that a number is associated with each possible response to a question. Instead of being asked, "What is your marital status?" respondents can be asked, "What is your marital status? Are you:

    (1) single, never married
    (2) married (first marriage)
    (3) remarried (second or subsequent)
    (4) divorced
    (5) widowed
    (6) other

In observational research, mechanical and electronic technologies have been developed for recording observational data so that further coding is unnecessary. These devices, which are used increasingly in marriage and family research, consist of a compact numeric keyboard that allows observers to rapidly key in codes for literally hundreds of behaviors as they occur. These observational coding machines are capable of storing a large amount of data in its exact behavioral sequence; later, these data can be transferred directly (electronically) to the computer.

Technical and technological advances have, fortunately, reduced the potential for error in time-consuming data preparation. Still, it pays to be sure that data are ready ("prepared") before being entered into the computer for analysis. Each case should have a unique identification number, and the data should be checked for double codes, illegible numerals, and simple mistakes.

There are several ways of entering data so that they can be processed by computers. Historically, coding sheets were taken to keypunch operators who punched the data onto 80-column cards that were then read electronically into the computer. Although cards can still be processed at some locations, the most common way of entering data now is by using a keyboard terminal with a screen. Instead of creating a physical punch card record of the data that is then read into the computer, *Direct Data Entry* (DDE) is a process of directly keying data into the computer from a terminal and storing them electronically. Other forms of streamlined data entry include optical scanning processors that read the location of pencil marks on special answer sheets. All of these forms of entering data for computer processing are used by marriage and family researchers.

DATA MANIPULATION
AND TRANSFORMATION

Once the raw data are accessible to the computer it is often necessary to manipulate them before the analyses can be conducted. Special programs might need to be written to arrange the data in a certain format, to sort cases in an order, or to merge and match more than one data file. The canned software programs (e.g., SPSS and SAS) most widely used by marriage and family researchers also have built in procedures for handling missing values, recoding variables, and creating new variables by performing arithmetic operations on variables in the file.

Missing Data

In most studies some cases will have missing data. Either on purpose or through oversight a respondent or interviewer will have left a question unanswered, or some observational data might have been lost. If there is a large amount of data missing for a case, it might be dropped from all analyses. Usually, however, only a small amount of data is missing for some cases and, given the efforts expended in data collection, it would be wasteful to exclude these cases entirely. In this situation the researchers can declare a "missing value" (or values) for each variable so that the computations include only cases with valid data. During the analyses cases with a declared missing value are temporarily set aside so that the missing data do not distort the results. This procedure allows analyses to be performed only on cases with valid data on the variable(s) being examined, without losing a case entirely.

Recoding Variables

It is strongly recommended that data be entered in their raw form, but for some analyses an investigator might want to look at a variable in a slightly different way. The variable "number of children" (ever born, living, or at home) will usually have been entered as a raw numeral, probably ranging from zero to 5, 6, or 7. In large-scale surveys and studies including high fertility groups (e.g., Hutterites, Mormons), the number of children should be coded as a two-digit variable (00, 05, 06, 07) so that the actual value can be included for parents with two digits' worth (10 or more) of children.

Recoding might be desirable if the investigator wants to consider not the actual number of children per se, but several salient categories such as: (1) those who have no children or only one (small families); (2) those who have 2 or 3 (roughly average); (3) those who have 4 or more (large families). This could be done by recoding the number of children variable so that 00 and 01 are set equal to 1, 02 and 03 equal to 2, and 04 through the largest number of children in the sample equal 3. From then on, the recoded number of children variable would have just three values—namely, small, medium, and large. The researcher would usually want this to be only a temporary procedure, though, because it might turn out to be critically important in the analyses to be able to go back to the raw data and see separately what subjects are like who have no children, or who have only one, or who have very many children (seven or more).

Constructing Variables

Marriage and family researchers frequently use variables that are constructed arithmetically. These constructed variables are of two main types. First, there are *composite indices* that combine several (or many) items intended to measure the same global construct (e.g., marital adjustment or sex-role orientation). Second, some constructed variables are not indexes or composite scales, but mathematical combinations of variables that are intended to operationalize an important marriage or family construct, such as rates or ratios.

Rates are, by definition, the number of occurrences per unit of the population. Because population bases will differ (comparing the same place at different times or different places at the same time) it is most useful to be able to compare not the total number of events (births, marriages, divorces), but the number of these events holding the population constant. Various marriage and family rates are commonly computed with formulas something like the following:

$$\frac{\text{number of births to}}{\text{15-19-year-old females}}{\text{total population}\atop\text{of 15-19-year-old females}} \times 1000$$

The result of this calculation is the 15-19-year-old fertility rate, or the number of births among 15-19-year-old females per 1000 15-19-year-old females in the population. This computed variable makes comparisons over time and between different places possible.

Sometimes marriage and family researchers are interested in ratio variables. In examining the effect of children on marriage, for example, it was hypothesized that there could be a kind of pile-up effect of having too many children too soon (Hurley and Palonen, 1967). This concept, called *child density,* required taking into account both number of children and time. Although an intuitively interesting constructed variable, simply dividing the number of children by years of marriage has not produced very noteworthy results (Figley, 1973; Miller, 1975).

Another issue in constructing variables has to do with the *unit of analysis.* In marriage and family studies a key variable might be some aspect of a couple's relationship that can only be understood by taking into account both husband and wife scores. Or, the constructed variables might reflect a property of the whole family created from the combined scores of various family members. When measuring couple or family group properties it might seem best to calculate an average score, or a discrepancy score, but this is both a conceptually and statistically complex issue (Schumm et al., 1985; Thomson and Williams, 1982; Tiggle et al., 1982).

Composite scales or indexes are very commonly used in marriage and family research. There are many ways to construct them, ranging from simple additive procedures to very complex weighting schemes that include several arithmetic operations. Constructing composite scales is really a measurement activity, but it can (and usually should) be done after raw data are on the computer, in advance of the actual statistical analyses.

STATISTICAL ANALYSES

In spite of the fact that they help to simplify and reduce data complexity, statistics intimidate many people. In fact, someone once said that "if all of the statisticians in the world were laid end to end, it would be a good thing." Statistics are just tools for understanding data. They are used in research to reduce the hundreds, thousands, or millions of separate bits of information to a more simple and interpretable form so that researchers can draw conclusions about the data. This section will present a very simple overview of statistics most commonly used in marriage and family research. A good way to gain further understanding would be to read one of the many statistics texts for the social-behavioral sciences. There are many technical complexities to the use and interpretation of statistics. For example, one of the oldest controversies is over whether or not more powerful statistical techniques with their stringent assumptions should be used on relatively weak nominal or ordinal-level data. In recent years, studies seem to have favored using strong statistics with weak data (Bollen and Barb, 1981; Labovitz, 1970, 1972). It takes considerable study, however, to use and understand more advanced statistical concepts, many of which are only barely mentioned here.

Univariate Analyses

Univariate means "one variable." Univariate statistics are sometimes also called *descriptive statistics* because they are used to describe a single variable. Descriptive statistics can be considered in three broad classes, namely, frequency distributions, measures of central tendency, and measures of dispersion.

Before beginning any complex statistical analysis, marriage and family researchers need to be able to describe what the important variables are like in the sample being studied. For example, if the number of children was a key variable in a study, it would make sense to generate a frequency distribution something like Table 6.1.

Table 6.1 describes the number of children in the sample in a rather simple and easily understood way. More respondents reported having two children (22%) or none (28%) than any other number. About equal proportions reported having one (14.8%), or three (15.8%) children. Decreasing percentages of respondents reported having four or more children. This simple table summarizes over 1500 responses in an efficient way. Although both raw numbers and percentages are given in Table 6.1, this is not always the case. Sometimes the same basic information is reported as a histogram (bar chart) or frequency poly-

TABLE 6.1
Number of Children for a Random Sample
of Americans 18 or Older
Who Are or Have Been Married

Number of Children	N	%
Zero	430	28.1
One	226	14.8
Two	349	22.8
Three	241	15.8
Four	132	8.6
Five	76	4.9
Six	28	1.8
Seven	17	1.1
Eight or more	31	2.0
	1530	100.0

SOURCE: Davis (1985).

gon. The most important data for descriptive purposes are the percentages rather than the raw number of cases.

Measures of central tendency express how the values of a variable are grouped together, or how the scores tend to cluster around a central, or average, value. There are three measures of central tendency: the mode, median, and mean. The *mode* is the most frequently occurring score (in Table 6.1 zero children is the mode). The *median* is the middle score; half of the scores are above and half below it (the median for Table 6.1 is 2.1). The *mean* is the arithmetic average obtained by summing all scores and dividing by the number of scores (in Table 6.1 the mean is 2.33 if all "eight or more" responses are treated as eight children). The mode is the only appropriate measure of central tendency for nominal-level data. The mean is generally preferred for continuous data (interval and ratio levels of measurement) except when there are extreme outlying scores. The median should be used if there are extreme scores in a distribution because these extreme scores will distort the mean (arithmetic average). Median family income is used in virtually all official reports, for example, because those with very high incomes would "pull up" the average income if the arithmetic mean was used.

Measures of dispersion tell how spread out scores are. These statistics are simple values or numbers (like the mode, median, and mean) that reflect how dispersed or spread out the scores are. The *range* is the simplest measure of dispersion or variability; it is the distance between lowest and highest scores. By far the most common measure of variability is the *standard deviation*. Given a mean score of central tendency, the standard deviation is the average (or standard) deviation of all raw scores from the mean. The larger the standard deviation, the more spread out, or dispersed, scores are from the mean. Most all marriage and family quantitative data analyses report, or at least use, univariate measures of central tendency and dispersion.

Bivariate Analyses

Bivariate means that two variables are examined or considered simultaneously. Bivariate or two variable relationships can sometimes be shown in tables that resemble the combination of simple frequency distributions. Table 6.2, for example, shows a relationship between the two variables of age when dating began and coital experience; more of those who began dating at young ages have experienced sexual intercourse.

Bivariate relationships are usually expressed in marriage and family studies, however, by a statistical measure of association that more concisely summarizes how two variables are related. A *measure of association* is a single value that expresses the strength of relationship between two variables. There are many statistical tests of the relationships between variables, and the choice of which one(s) to use depends on level of measurement of the variables. A correlation is expressed as a single coefficient of association that ranges between plus and minus one. The larger the correlation coefficient, the more strongly two variables are related. In addition to the strength of a relationship that is reflected by the size of the correlation coefficient, the direction of

TABLE 6.2
Relationship Between Age When Dating Began
and Adolescent Coital Experiences

Experienced Sexual Intercourse	*Age at Which Dating Began*						
	12	13	14	15	16	17	
Yes	90.9	52.6	49.3	38.8	17.4	12.5	
No	9.1	47.4	50.7	61.2	82.6	87.5	
Totals (%)	100	100	100	100	100	100	
n	(11)	(38)	(67)	(134)	(172)	(8)	(430)

SOURCE: Miller et al. (1986). Reprinted by permission.

relationships is also important. A positive association means that the variables vary in the same direction (e.g., as verbal aggression increases, so does physical violence); a negative association means that the variables vary in opposite directions (e.g., as length of marriage increases, frequency of sexual intercourse declines).

Multivariate Analyses

Multivariate analyses simultaneously include three or more variables. Multivariate techniques are used in many ways because most research questions involve more than just one or two variables. The number and complexity of multivariate techniques are far beyond the scope of this book, although a few conceptual examples will be presented. Nearly all statistics texts include multivariate statistical analyses, and some texts (Tabachnick and Fidell, 1983) are specifically written to help researchers understand multivariate statistics.

Factor analysis is a multivariate statistical procedure (actually a group of related procedures) that is widely used to reduce a large set of variables to a smaller number of underlying dimensions. In scale or instrument development, factor analysis is used to see how the items related to one another could be grouped to form subscales that are theoretically interesting and empirically justified. Within a set of items designed to measure dyadic adjustment, for example, factors such as consensus, satisfaction, and cohesion are clearly evident in the way that individual items are related to each other (Spanier and Thompson, 1982).

Cluster analysis is another multivariate statistical procedure that is conceptually similar to factor analysis (Bailey, 1975). However, instead of grouping together items or variables into factors, cluster analysis groups together objects (individuals, couples, families) being studied according to their similarities on the variables in the analysis (Mezzich and Solomon, 1980). For example, types of couple interaction have been identified by clustering together marital pairs who interacted in similar ways (Miller and Olson, 1979; Olson, 1981).

A different set of multivariate procedures are appropriate when multiple independent variables are used to predict a single dependent measure. Using path analysis, the direct and indirect (through other variables) effects of multiple independent variables on a single dependent variable have been estimated in a variety of marriage and family research questions (Schumm et al., 1980). Thornton and Camburn

(1983) reported that only a selected subset of family background and relationship variables included in multiple regression analyses were predictive of adolescent sexual attitudes and behavior. There are conceptually similar multivariate techniques that are used when the independent variables are measured categorically (multivariate analysis of variance) or when the dependent variable being predicted is categorical (discriminant analysis). Multivariate statistics have also been recommended to family researchers when their problem is to consider simultaneously the relationships between multiple independent variables and multiple dependent variables (McLauglin and Otto, 1981).

This part of the chapter could go on almost indefinitely telling how various types of innovative and emergent multivariate statistical techniques have been used in marriage and family research (Acock, 1979; Joreskog, 1969, 1973, 1979). Suffice it to say that many marriage and family issues of interest to researchers are multivariate in nature; that is, marriage and family phenomena are rarely (perhaps never) associated with, or the result of, only one independent variable. Primarily for this reason, but also because it has become technically more feasible, multivariate analyses are the current standard in quantitative marriage and family research.

STATISTICAL SIGNIFICANCE

One of the ways statistics are used in research is to assist in making decisions about the significance of results. Scientific decision making has come to rely on a set of rules or statistical conventions known as significance testing. Tests of statistical significance are used when researchers want to make inferences (or decisions) about populations based on only a sample of data taken from the population. Samples, of course, differ from each other and from the population that they represent. Statistical significance helps researchers infer (or decide) whether there is a difference between groups (e.g., a difference in activity levels of male and female infants), or if there is a relationship between variables (e.g., the length of marriage and marital role segregation).

The null hypothesis has a particularly important role in statistical decision theory. The primary convention is to minimize the probability of falsely rejecting the null hypothesis. Rejecting a null hypothesis when it should not have been is called making a Type 1, or alpha, error. The generally accepted statistical rule of thumb is that a type 1 (alpha) error should be made no more than 5% or 1% of the time. In other words, the most common probability, or p level, is .05 or .01. When statistical tests show a probability of less than .05 (.008, for example) results are considered "statistically significant" and researchers are relatively confident about rejecting the null hypothesis in favor of the alternate hypothesis that there is a significant difference or relationship.

SUMMARY

Data analyses are planned and carried out to answer specific research questions. Before statistics can be computed, however, it is important to take several preliminary steps to maximize data quality. These preliminary steps sometimes include coding data into a desired format, entering the data so they are accessible to the computer, locating, designating or otherwise treating missing values, and recoding and transforming variables so that they are accurate operationalizations of the concepts being studied.

Statistical analyses usually begin with simple one-variable (univariate) descriptions so that the key variables under study are clearly understood. Frequency distributions will be calculated for the dependent and independent variable(s). Two-variable (bivariate) relationships can be assessed by various measures of association that summarize the direction and strength of their relationship.

In many contemporary marriage and family studies, multivariate statistical techniques are used. Multivariate techniques are technical and complex, but they most closely approach the reality of marriage and family phenomena that are influenced by many variables.

Tests of statistical significance are used to decide when results obtained with a sample are really worth paying attention to.

KEY CONCEPTS

Case
Coding
Data entry
Recoding
Missing values

Variable transformations
Statistics
Univariate
    Frequency distribution
    Central tendency
    Dispersion
Bivariate
    Measures of association
    Negative relationship
    Positive relationship
    Strength of relationship
Multivariate
    Statistical control
Statistical significance

CHAPTER

7

Conclusions and Implications

There is still no man who would not accept dog tracks in the mud against the testimony of a hundred eye witnesses that no dog had passed by.

W. L. Prosser

AFTER THE DATA HAVE BEEN ANALYZED in ways that would answer the original research questions or test the hypotheses, the investigator is faced with interpreting the results. What do the results mean? How generalizable are the conclusions that can be drawn? If they differ from what was expected, why? What are the implications of the study for theory, for further research, for application? What were the limitations of the study? These are some of the issues that will be considered in this final chapter.

INTERPRETING WHAT THE FINDINGS MEAN

In family research reports "Results" or "Findings" sections sometimes are followed by a section called the "Discussion." In other reports the "Results and Discussion" are combined in presentation. In any case, virtually every report will include a section in which the findings of the study are considered in light of what was expected. After all, the study was undertaken for some reason, possibly to answer a specific question or to test hypotheses. In light of these conceptual beginnings, what do the findings mean?

In the simplest case, if the study tested a single hypothesis using only one measure, it should be possible to draw conclusions quickly and easily. Whether to reject a null hypothesis that there was no difference between groups or no relationship between the independent and dependent variables could be readily apparent from the statistical analyses conducted. If age had been related to sex-role orientations (Brogan and Kutner, 1976), for example, and if the average sex-role orientation scores were 175, 160, and 143 for those younger than 23, those 23-45, and over 45, respectively, and if the statistical analysis showed that these differences were statistically significant, then the null hypothesis of no age difference in sex-role orientation would be rejected. The observed mean scores could be interpreted as evidence supporting the conclusion that age is related to sex-role orientations, with older persons being more traditional.

Rather than *proving* that age is related to sex-role orientations, however, the results of this or any other single study should generally be interpreted more conservatively. The pattern of results described above could more appropriately be interpreted as evidence (rather than "proof") supporting the conclusions that age is related to sex-role orientations, with older persons being more traditional. This more tentative conclusion would be particularly appropriate in the above example because the relationship between age and sex-role orientation barely attained statistical significance by usual standards (p = .04) and the same relationship among women was not quite significant (p = .07).

In many cases the analyses will have included several tests of the relationship being studied but using different measures. In such cases, the task of the researcher is to interpret the pattern of results obtained with different operationalizations of the key variables, perhaps among samples with different characteristics, or in different locations, and so on. In sum, the interpretation of research results is usually not so simple and straightforward as it tends to be presented in textbook examples.

After the data have been interpreted and conclusions drawn, there are still several issues that deserve to be considered. These include limitations of the study, generalizability of the results, and implications of the research.

LIMITATIONS OF THE STUDY

This book generally has described an ideal of how family research would be conducted if the real world would just relax and cooperate. In actual practice, however, the ideal of orderly research is difficult to carry out; instead of neatness and order, research is messy and inclined toward mistakes and errors. Every study has limitations because of what happened that should not have or what should have happened that did not. It is an accepted convention (and it seems only proper) to state caveats and disclaimers as the "limitations of the study."

Unexpected problems that compromise or limit the research can be encountered at virtually any stage of the process. The measures might not perform as expected or be defective in some way. After administering a long survey to several hundred subjects an investigator might discover that the typist who prepared the final draft had left out one item of a standardized scale. A researcher might repeatedly arrange group meetings for new parents as part of an experimental treatment, only to have them repeatedly not show up. A sampling plan that is supposed to produce a large enough sample for analyses of subgroups can somehow come up short. (These examples come from personal experiences.) One eminent family scholar told how he had discovered through selective telephone calls to subjects that the completed interviews turned in by one interviewer had never taken place. A highly visible but totally unexpected event (a big news story, a Supreme Court decision, law, or policy) can occur that has an important bearing on the respondents' answers or behavior. There are, in short, innumerable reasons for a study to have limitations.

Some studies are not beset with the kinds, or perhaps the magnitude, of problems described above. A statement of limitations is still usually called for, however, because no single study can claim to be definitive. A study that is well done is still limited to the specific operationalizations of the variables that were used; if things had been measured differently the results might have changed. If the study were done with other subjects different results might also have been obtained. These latter caveats raise the issue of generalizability of the results.

GENERALIZABILITY OF RESULTS

Generalizability has to do with how widely the findings apply or might hold. To what other populations of subjects, situations, and measures can the observed results be applied? There are several general principles that govern generalizability of findings.

First, generalizability is reduced to the extent that the subjects are unlike those in the population of interest. The question of whether or not the findings will generalize to different populations must await studies of those populations. This is why so much emphasis is placed on drawing samples of populations that can be considered truly representative. An investigator can only generalize from sample findings to the population if the former represents the latter.

Similarly, if a relationship is found in an artificial setting such as a laboratory, its generalizability can only be shown by the extent to which it (the relationship) also can be found in more naturalistic environments.

Finally, generalizability must be considered with respect to the particular measures used in the study. Would the results obtained have been similar if the investigator had used a different measure of the same variables? Some relationships are strong enough to show up despite different ways of measuring the phenomena of interest.

In sum, the issue of generalizability requires the investigator to consider the extent to which what he or she has found is a general principle that is not limited to a particular kind of subject, place, or measure.

IMPLICATIONS OF THE RESEARCH

Writing the implications of a study is kind of like being asked, "What's the bottom line?" or "How can the results be used?"

Implications for Theory

The results of empirical studies often have implications for the revision, refinement, or verification of theories. Some philosophers of science take a much firmer position about the relationship between research and theory. Karl Popper, for example, asserted in a classic argument (1965) that theories can be refined *only* by empirical refutations of incorrect conjectures. If a study is conducted so that conclusions can be drawn, it is almost sure to have implications for theory. Unfortunately, investigators do not always realize this or they do not make the effort to spell out how the results of their work impinge on theory.

It is an indication of excellence when researchers carefully identify the theoretical ideas behind their empirical work and, after the results are in, then spell out the theoretical implications of what has been found. For example, Acock and Bengtson (1980) received a national award from their peers in recognition of their study that integrated research and theory in the analysis of parent-child socialization. They found that children's *perceptions* of parents were more influential in explaining child outcomes than *actual* parental reports, and they argued that these results are most consistent with a theory that gives a central place to the importance of perceptions.

Implications for Research

Much like the theoretical implications that follow from a well-executed study, there are often implications for future research. One kind of research implication arising from a completed study basically states how the methodological conduct of the investigation could be improved. In other words, certain problems and their consequent limitations in one study can be avoided in future work if the pitfalls are clearly identified.

On the other hand, an especially promising aspect of a methodological procedure might be recommended to other investigators. The Revealed Difference Technique developed by Strodtbeck (1951) in the course of a specific study of husband and wife power, for example, had important implications for measurement approaches used in later studies of marital power and conflict (Olson and Ryder, 1970). Methodological recommendations are often made as a result of using some relatively new techniques in the study of marriages or families. Examples range from apparently promising approaches to data collection (Gelles, 1984) to apparently useful new measurement scales (Wampler and Powell, 1982) to techniques for data analysis (Acock, 1979; McLaughlin and Otto, 1981; Sackett, 1978).

A third kind of implication for future research is substantive in nature. Sometimes research questions emerge or come into sharper focus as a consequence of a study. As mentioned previously, new hypotheses often are generated in the course of conducting research. In this case, the implications for future investigations pose research questions that need to be addressed by additional studies.

In summary, many implications for future research can follow from a given study. Research implications might point out pitfalls to be avoided, procedures or techniques that are thought to be particularly promising, or substantive issues that appear to be deserving of further investigation.

Implications for Practice

As I pointed out in Chapter 1, basic or pure research is conducted in pursuit of knowledge about marriages and families. Sometimes basic research findings turn out to have important implications for practitioners. For example, classical learning principles that were first investigated by psychologists around the turn of the century and operant learning principles refined in more recent decades have had immense practical implications for the behavioral treatment of individual disorders and for marital and family therapy.

More applied studies are sometimes sponsored specifically to obtain research data that can be used to help make practical or programmatic decisions. Research that evaluates educational programs like Operation Head Start or other types of prevention or intervention programs has practical implications for how those programs will be conducted in the future. Family life educators (Miller et al., 1981), marriage and family therapists, and family social service workers make up the largest groups of practitioners who are benefited by research that is conducted with a sensitivity for its practical applications.

A FINAL NOTE ABOUT
MARRIAGE AND FAMILY RESEARCH

By now it should be obvious that marriage and family research is not an exact or precise science. There is plenty of reason for marriage and family scholars to be modest about what they know and humble about what they do not (Doherty, 1984). The subject matter consists, after all, of some of the most private, personally valued, complex, and deliberately disguised of human behaviors.

On the other hand, marriage and family research is not a mystical or arm-chair activity. For the most part, marriage and family researchers collectively are engaged in serious attempts to describe and explain empirical patterns and general principles. As introduced in this book, their efforts include a diverse array of research methods. And this small text has barely scratched the surface; it omits entirely econometric methods (Becker, 1981), ethnographic procedures (Murdock and Schlegel, 1980), content analysis and diary study (Walker and Woods, 1976), as well as many other methodological topics. Research methods are important—not as ends in themselves—but for what they are able to help us understand about marriages and families.

Abraham Kaplan (1964), in an older work about the behavioral sciences, wrote a description that applies neatly to family researchers and their methods:

> Every scientific community is a society in the small, so to speak, with its own agencies of social control. Officers of the professional associations, honored elders, editors of journals, reviewers, faculties, committees on grants, fellowships, and prizes—all exert a steady pressure for conformity to professional standards. . . . The innate conservatism, or at least inertia, of professional standards has from time to time stood in the way of scientific progress. The martyrs of science have sometimes been victims of the faithful rather than of the infidels. . . . Yet for every resisted scientific genius there are numberless crackpots. . . . Standards of scientific excellence, though they may occasionally be self-defeating, on the whole and in the long run make for success. Adherence to the Law is the surest, and perhaps the only, safeguard against being misled by false Prophets [Kaplan, 1964: 4, 5].

The "Law" in family research is not as crystalized or supreme as implied by the above quote, even though some researchers do become overly awed by and dependent on their techniques. There are, however, research methods to be acquired and taken advantage of in trying to better understand marriage and family behavior. Techniques and technologies cannot conceptualize and ask questions, however. There is no substitute for good ideas and clear thinking. Advances in marriage and family scholarship are most likely to occur when those who can most clearly conceptualize theoretical questions have also mastered methodological skills.

SUMMARY

An empirical study is not complete until the analysis of data has been interpreted and conclusions drawn. The task of interpretation is to try and make sense out of the pattern of results. More often than not, some results will suggest one interpretation whereas others are inconclusive or even contradictory.

In marriage and family research—as in empirical studies of any kind—there are limitations. These should be acknowledged and drawn to the attention of potential readers so that similar difficulties can be avoided in the future. There are also limitations that are not a result of specific problems encountered but that are based on the fact that no one study can stand alone. Family investigations usually are restricted or limited by their cultural context, sample characteristics, having measures of only one or two kinds, and so on.

Every well-done study has implications, usually of several kinds. Implications from research might include evidence that a theory should be revised, discarded, or elaborated in some way to take account of the new information. Virtually every study will have implications for the conduct of future research; research implications might include mistakes to be avoided, new techniques that appear to be promising, and the emergence of additional related questions that could be addressed. Research sometimes has implications for applied use by practitioners. The knowledge gained by even so-called pure or basic research might at some future time come to be important in practical applications.

Marriage and family research is a search for meaning, under-standing, and knowledge. The research methods used should be viewed as a means to that end rather than as an end in themselves. Family research methods are important tools that should only be used when guided by clear and logical thought.

KEY CONCEPTS

Interpreting findings
Evidence versus proof
Limitations
Generalizability
Theoretical implications
Research implications
Practical implications

References

ACOCK, A. C. (1979) "Applications of LISREL IV to family research." Presented at preconference theory and methods workshop, National Council on Family Relations, Boston.

———and V. L. BENGTSON (1980) "Socialization and attribution processes: actual versus perceived similarity among parents and youth." Journal of Marriage and the Family 42: 501-516.

ADAMS, G. R. and J. D. SCHVANEVELDT (1985) Understanding Research Methods. New York: Longman.

ALDOUS, J. (1978) Family Careers: Developmental Change in Families. New York: John Wiley.

ALTHAUSER, R. P. and T. A. HEBERLEIN (1970) Validity and the multitrait-multimethod matrix. In E. F. Borgatta and G. W. Bohrnstedt (Eds.), Sociological Methodology (pp. 151-169), San Francisco: Jossey-Bass.

American Psychological Association (1973) Ethical principles in the conduct of research with human participants. Washington, DC: Author.

American Sociological Association (1968) Toward a code of ethics for sociologists. American Sociologist 3: 316-318.

ANASTASI, A. (1976) Psychological Testing. New York: Macmillan.

BAILEY, K. D. (1975) "Cluster analysis," in D. Heise (ed.) Sociological Methodology. San Francisco: Jossey-Bass.

BALES, R. F. (1950) Interaction Process Analysis: A Method for the Study of Small Groups. Cambridge, MA: Addison-Mosley.

BAUMRIND, D. (1980) "New directions in socialization research." American Psychologist 35: 639-652.

BECKER, G. S. (1981) A Treatise on the Family. Cambridge, MA: Harvard University Press.

BELSKY, L., G. B. SPANIER and M. ROVINE (1983) "Stability and change in marriage across the transition to parenthood." Journal of Marriage and the Family 45: 576-577.

BLAKE, J. (1981) "Family size and the quality of children." Demography 18: 421-422.

BLALOCK, H. M. (1979) "Measurement and conceptualization problems: the major obstacle to integrated theory and research." American Sociological Review 44: 881-894.

———(1982) Conceptualization and Measurement in the Social Sciences. Beverly Hills, CA: Sage.

BOHRNSTEDT, G. W. (1983) "Measurement," in P. Rossi et al. (eds.) Handbook of Survey Research. New York: Academic.
———and E. F. BORGATTA (1981) Social Measurement. Beverly Hills, CA: Sage.
BOLLEN, K. A. and K. H. BARB (1981) "Pearson's R and coarsely categorized measures." American Sociological Review 46: 232-239.
BONJEAN, C. M., R. J. HILL, and S. D. McLEMORE (1967) Sociological Measurement: An Inventory of Scales and Indices. San Francisco: Chandler.
BOWERMAN, C. E. (1964) "Prediction studies," in H. T. Christensen (ed.) Handbook of Marriage and the Family. Chicago: Rand-McNally.
———and J. W. KINCH (1959) "Changes in family and peer orientation of children between the fourth and tenth grades." Social Forces 37: 206-211.
BRODY, G. H. and R. C. ENDSLEY (1981) "Researching children and families: differences in approaches of child and family specialists." Family Relations 30: 275-280.
BROGAN, D. and N. G. KUTNER (1976) "Measuring sex role orientation: a normative approach." Journal of Marriage and the Family 38: 31-40.
BURGESS, E. W. and P. WALLIN (1953) Engagement and Marriage. Philadelphia: Lippincott.
BUROS, O. K. (1972) Seventh Mental Measurements Yearbook. Highland Park, NJ: Gryphone Press.
———(1974) Tests in Print II. Highland Park, NJ: Gryphone Press.
BURR, W. R. (1973) Theory Construction and the Sociology of the Family. New York: John Wiley.
———and G. K. LEIGH (1983) "Famology: A new discipline." Journal of Marriage and the Family 45: 467-480.
BURR, W. R., R. HILL, F. I. NYE, and I. L. REISS (1979) Contemporary Theories about the Family (vols. 1 and 2). New York: Free Press.
CALL, V.R.A., L. B. OTTO, and K. I. SPENNER (1982) Tracking Respondents: A Multimethod Approach. Lexington, MA: D. C. Heath.
CAMPBELL, D. T. and D. W. FISKE (1959) "Convergent and discriminant validation by the multitrait-multimethod matrix." Psychological Bulletin 56: 81-105.
CAMPBELL, D. T. and J. C. STANLEY (1963) "Experimental and quasi-experimental designs for research on teaching," in N. L. Gage (ed.) Handbook of Research on Teaching. Chicago: Rand-McNally.
CAMPBELL, A., P. E. CONVERSE, and W. L. RODGERS (1976) The quality of American life. New York: Russell Sage.
CAPLOW, T., H. M. BAHR, B. A. CHADWICK, R. HILL, and M. H. WILLIAMSON (1982) Middletown Families. Minneapolis: University of Minnesota.
CARMINES, E. G. and R. A. ZELLER (1979) Reliability and Validity Assessment. Beverly HIlls, CA: Sage.
CHERLIN, A. (1977) "The effects of children on marital dissolution." Demography 14: 265-272.
CHRISTENSEN, H. T. (1963) "Child spacing analysis via record linkage: new data plus a summing up from earlier reports." Marriage and Family Living 25: 272-280.
———(1964) "Development of the family field of study," in H. T. Christensen (ed.) Handbook of Marriage and the Family. Chicago: Rand-McNally.

CHUN, K., S. COBB, and R. P. FRENCH, Jr. (1975) Measures for Psychological Assessment. Ann Arbor: University of Michigan.

COHEN, J. A. (1960) "A coefficient of agreement for nominal scales." Educational and Psychological Measurement 20: 37-46.

COOK, T. D. and D. T. CAMPBELL (1979) Quasi-Experimentation: Design and Analysis Issues for Field Settings. Chicago: Rand-McNally.

CROMWELL, R. E. and D. C. FOURNIER (forthcoming) Diagnosing Relationships: A Measurement Handbook for Marital and Family Therapists. San Francisco: Jossey-Bass.

CROMWELL, R. E., D. M. KLEIN, and S. G. WEITING (1975) "Family power: a multitrait-multimethod analysis," in R. E. Cromwell and D. M. Klein (eds.) Power in Families. Beverly Hills, CA: Sage.

CRONBACH, L. J. (1951) "Coefficient alpha and the internal structure of tests." Psychometrika 16: 297-334.

CRONBACH, L. J. and P. MEEHL (1955) "Construct validity of psychological tests." Psychological Bulletin 2: 181-302.

———C. G. GLASER, H. NANDA, and N. RAJARATNAM (1972) The Dependability of Behavioral Measurements: Theory of Generalizability for Scores and Profiles. New York: John Wiley.

CUBER, J. F. and P. B. HARROFF (1965) The Significant Americans: A Study of Sexual Behavior Among the Affluent. New York: Van Rees Press.

DAVIS, J. A. (1985) General Social Surveys, 1972-1985: Cumulative Codebook. Chicago: National Opinion Research Center.

DIENER, E. and R. CRANDALL (1978) Ethics in Social and Behavioral Research. Chicago: University of Chicago Press.

DILLMAN, D. A. (1978) Mail and Telephone Surveys: The Total Design Method. New York: John Wiley.

DIZARD, J. (1968) Social Change in the Family. Chicago: Community and Family Center, University of Chicago.

DOHERTY, W. J. (1984) "Quanta, quarks, and families: implications of modern physics for studying families." Presented at the Theory and Methods Preconference Workshop, National Council on Family Relations.

DURKHEIM, E. (1951) Suicide: A Study in Sociology. [John A. Spaulding and George Simpson, trans.] New York: Free Press.

DUSTER, T., D. MATZA, and D. WELLMAN (1979) "Field work and the protection of human subjects." American Sociologist 14: 136-142.

ELDER, G. H. (1981) "History and the family: the discovery of complexity." Journal of Marriage and the Family 43: 489-514.

ELDER, G. H., Jr. (1974) Children of the Great Depression. Chicago: University of Chicago Press.

ETAUGH, C. and J. MALSTROM (1981) "The effect of marital status on person perception." Journal of Marriage and the Family 4: 801-805.

FELDMAN, H. (1971) "The effects of children on the family," in A. Michael (ed.) Family Issues of Employed Women in Europe and America. Leiden, The Netherlands: E. J. Brill.

FIGLEY, C. R. (1973) "Child density and the marital relationship." Journal of Marriage and the Family 35: 272-282.

FILSINGER, E. E. (1981) "The dyadic interaction scoring code," in E. E. Filsinger and R. A. Lewis (eds.) Assessing Marriage: New Behavioral Approaches. Beverly Hills, CA: Sage.
———and R. A. LEWIS (1981) Assessing Marriage: New Behavioral Approaches. Beverly Hills, CA: Sage.
FOURNIER, D. G., D. H. OLSON, and J. M. DRUCKMAN (1983) "Assessing marital and premarital relationships: the PREPARE-ENRICH Inventories," in E. E. Filsinger (ed.) Marriage and Family Assessment. Beverly Hills, CA: Sage.
FOWERS, B. J. and D. H. OLSON (n.d.) "Predicting marital success with PREPARE: a predictive validity study." Unpublished manuscript, Department of Family Social Science, University of Minnesota.
FREEDMAN, D. S., A. THORNTON, and D. CAMBURN (1980) "Maintaining response rates in longitudinal studies." Sociological Methods and Research 9: 87-98.
FURSTENBERG, F. F., Jr. (1985) "Sociological ventures in child development." Child Development 56: 281-288.
GECAS, V. (1971) "Parental behavior and adolescent self-evaluation." Sociometry 34: 466-482.
GELLES, R. J. (1974) The Violent Home: A Study of Physical Aggression Between Husbands and Wives. Beverly Hills, CA: Sage.
———(1984) "Parental child snatching: a preliminary estimate of the national incidence." Journal of Marriage and the Family 45: 735-739.
GERGEN, K. J. (1982) Toward Transformation in Social Knowledge. New York: Springer-Verlag.
GLENN, N. D. and S. McLANAHAN (1982) "Children and marital happiness: a further specification of the relationship." Journal of Marriage and the Family 44: 63-72.
GLICK, P. C. (1964) "Demographic analysis of family data," in H. T. Christensen (ed.) Handbook of Marriage and the Family. Chicago: Rand-McNally.
GOFFMAN, E. (1983) "The interaction order." American Sociological Review 48: 1-17.
GOODRICH, D. W. and D. S. BOOMER (1963) "Experimental assessment of modes of conflict resolution." Family Process 2: 15-24.
GOTTMAN, J. M. (1979) Marital Interaction: Experimental Investigations. New York: Academic.
GOYDER, J. C. (1982) "Further evidence on factors affecting response rates to mailed questionnaires." American Sociological Review 47: 550-553.
GREENBLAT, C. S. (1983) "The salience of sexuality in the early years of marriage." Journal of Marriage and the Family 45: 289-300.
GROVES, R. M. and R. L. KAHN (1979) Surveys by Telephone: A National Comparison with Personal Interviews. New York: Academic.
HEBERLEIN, T. A. and R. BAUMGARTNER (1978) "Factors affecting response rates to mailed questionnaires: a quantitative analysis of the published literature." American Sociological Review 43: 447-462.
HERSEN, M. and D. H. DARLOW (1976) Single Case Experimental Designs: Strategies for Studying Behavior Change. New York: Pergamon.
HILL, R. (1964) "Methodological issues in family development research." Family Process 3: 186-206.
———and P. MATTESSICH (1979) "Family development theory and life span development," in P. B. Baltes and O. G. Brim (eds.) Life Span Development and Behavior (vol. 2). New York: Academic.

HODGSON, J. W. and R. A. LEWIS (1979) "Pilgrim's progress III: a trend analysis of family theory and methodology." Family Process 18: 163-173.

HOWARD, R. L. (1981) A Social History of American Family Sociology, 1865-1940. Westport, CT: Greenwood Press.

HURLEY, J. R. and D. P. PALONEN (1967) "Marital satisfaction and child density among university student parents." Journal of Marriage and the Family 29: 483-484.

HUSTON, T., S. McHALE, and A. CROUTER (1985) "When the honeymoon's over: changes in marriage over the first year," in S. Tuck and R. Gilmour (eds.) The Emerging Field of Personal Relationships. Hillsdale, NJ: Lawrence Erlbaum.

HYMAN, H. H. (1972) Secondary Analysis of Sample Surveys: Principles, Procedures, and Potentialities. New York: John Wiley.

Institute for Social Research (1976) Interviewers Manual (2nd ed.). Ann Arbor: University of Michigan.

Institute for Social Research (ISR) Newsletter (1981, Winter) "Rensis Likert: a final tribute." Pp. 6-7.

JOHNSON, O. G. and J. W. BOMMARITO (1971) Tests and Measurements in Child Development: A Handbook. San Francisco: Jossey-Bass.

JORDAN, L. A., A. C. MARCUS, and L. G. REEDER (1980) "Response styles in telephone and household interviewing: a field experiment." Public Opinion Quarterly 44: 210-222.

JÖRESKOG, K. G. (1969) "A general approach to confirmatory maximum likelihood factor analysis." Psychometrika 34: 183-202.

———(1973) "A general method for estimating a linear structural equation system," in A. S. Goldberger and O. D. Duncan (eds.) Structural Equation Models in the Social Sciences. New York: Seminar Press.

———(1979) Addendum to "A general approach to confirmatory maximum likelihood factor analysis," in Advances in Factor Analysis and Structural Equation Models. Cambridge, MA: Abt.

KAATS, G. R. and K. E. DAVIS (1970) "The dynamics of sexual behavior in college students." Journal of Marriage and the Family 32: 390-399.

KANTOR, D. H. and W. LEHR (1975) Inside the Family. San Francisco: Jossey-Bass.

KAPLAN, A. (1964) The Conduct of Inquiry. San Francisco: Chandler.

KENKEL, W. F. and D. K. HOFFMAN (1956) "Real and conceived roles in family decision making." Marriage and Family Living 18: 311-316.

KERLINGER, F. N. (1973) Foundations of Behavioral Research (2nd ed.). New York: Holt, Rinehart, & Winston.

———(1979) Behavioral Research: A conceptual Approach. New York: Holt, Rinehart, & Winston.

KIDWELL, J. S. (1982) "The neglected birth order: middleborns." Journal of Marriage and the Family 44: 225-235.

KITSON, G. C., M. B. SUSSMAN, G. K. WILLIAMS, R. B. ZEEHANDELAAR, B. K. SCHICKMANTER, and J. L. STEINBERGER (1982) "Sampling issues in family research." Journal of Marriage and the Family 44 (November): 965-981.

KLECKA, W. R. and A. J. TUCHFARBER (1978) "Random digit dialing: a comparison to personal surveys." Public Opinion Quarterly 42: 105-114.

KLEIN, D. M., S. R. JORGENSEN, and B. C. MILLER (1978) "Research methods and developmental reciprocity in families," in R. M. Lerner and G. B. Spanier (eds.) Child Influences on Marital and Family Interaction: A Life Span Perspective. New York: Academic.

KLEIN, D. M., J. D. SCHVANEVELDT, and B. C. MILLER (1978) "The attitudes and activities of contemporary family theorists." Journal of Comparative Family Studies 8: 5-17.

KRUSKAL, J. B. and M. WISH (1978) Multidimensional Scaling. Beverly Hills, CA: Sage.

LABOVITZ, S. (1970) "The assignment of numbers to rank order categories." American Sociological Review 35: 515-524.

———(1972) "Statistical usage in sociology: sacred cows and rituals." Sociological Methods and Research 1: 13-37.

LAKE, D. B., M. B. MILES, and R. B. EARLE (1973) Measuring Human Behavior. New York: Teachers College Press.

LAMB, M. E., L. J. SUOMI, and G. R. STEPHENSON [Eds.] (1979) Social Interactional Analysis: Methodological Issues. Madison: University of Wisconsin Press.

LaROSSA, R. and M. M. LaROSSA (1981) Transition to Parenthood. Beverly Hills, CA: Sage.

LaROSSA, R. and J. H. WOLF (1985) "Qualitative family research." Journal of Marriage and the Family 47: 531-541.

LaROSSA, R., L. A. BENNETT, and R. J. GELLES (1981) "Ethical dilemmas in qualitative family research." Journal of Marriage and the Family 43: 303-313.

LARZELERE, R. E. and D. M. KLEIN (forthcoming) "Methodological implications of the family as an object of study," in M. B. Sussman and S. K. Steinmetz (eds.) Handbook of Marriage and the Family. New York: Plenum Press.

LASLETT, P. [Ed.] (1972) Household and Family in Past Time. Cambridge, England: Cambridge University Press.

LePLAY, F. (1855) Les Ouvriers Europeens. Tours, France: Alfred Mame et Fils.

LIKER, J. K. and G. H. ELDER, Jr. (1983) "Economic hardship and marital relations in the 1930's." American Sociological Review 48: 343-359.

LIKERT, R. (1932) "A technique for the measurement of attitudes." Archives of Psychology 21, 140.

LODGE, M. (1981) Magnitude Scaling: Quantitative Measurement of Opinions. Beverly Hills, CA: Sage.

MANGEN, D. J. and W. A. PETERSON (1982a) Research Instruments in Social Gerontology: (vol. 1). Clinical and Social Psychology. Minneapolis: University of Minnesota Press.

———(1982b) Research Instruments in Social Gerontology: (vol. 2). Social Roles and Social Participation. Minneapolis: University of Minnesota Press.

MARANELL, G. M. (1974) Scaling: A Sourcebook for Behavioral Scientists. Hawthorne, NY: Aldine.

MARKMAN, H. J., C. I. NOTARIUM, T. STEPHEN, and R. J. SMITH (1981) "Behavioral observation systems for couples: the current status," in E. E. Filsinger and R. A. Lewis (eds.) Assessing Marriage: New Behavioral Approaches. Beverly Hills, CA: Sage.

McIVER, J. P. and E. G. CARMINES (1981) Unidimensional Scaling. Beverly Hills, CA: Sage.

McLAUGHLIN, S. D. and L. B. OTTO (1981) "Canonical correlation analysis in family research." Journal of Marriage and the Family 43: 7-16.

MEZZICH, J. E. and H. SOLOMON (1980) Taxonomy and Behavioral Science. New York: Academic.

MILLER, B. C. (1975) "Child density, marital satisfaction, and conventionalization: a research note." Journal of Marriage and the Family 2: 345-347.

———(1976) "A multivariate developmental model of marital satisfaction." Journal of Marriage and the Family 38: 643-657.

———and S. L. BOWEN (1982) "Father-to-newborn attachment behavior in relation to prenatal classes and presence at delivery." Family Relations 31: 71-78.

MILLER, B. C., J. K. McCOY, and T. D. OLSON (1986) "Dating experiences in relation to adolescent sexual attitudes and behavior." Unpublished manuscript.

MILLER, B. C. and D. H. OLSON (1979) "Types of marital interaction and related contextual characteristics: cluster analysis of the IMC." Presented at a conference on exploring styles in family systems, St. Paul, Minnesota.

MILLER, B. C., B. C. ROLLINS, and D. L. THOMAS (1982) "On methods of studying marriages and families." Journal of Marriage and the Family 44: 851-873.

MILLER, B. C., J. D. SCHVANEVELDT, and G. O. JENSON (1981) "Reciprocity between family life research and education." Family Relations 30: 625-630.

MILLER, B. C. and D. L. SOLLIE (1980) "Normal stresses during the transition to parenthood." Family Relations 29: 459-465.

MILLER, D. C. (1970) Handbook of Research Design and Social Measurement (2nd ed.). New York: David McKay.

MISHLER, E. G., and N. E. WAXLER (1966) "Family interaction and schizophrenia." Archives of General Psychiatry 15: 64-74.

MURDOCK, B. H. and A. SCHLEGEL (1980) Cross Cultural Samples and Codes. Pittsburgh: University of Pittsburgh Press.

National Opinion Research Corporation (1978) General Social Science Survey Codebook. Chicago: Author.

NUNNALLY, J. C. (1978) Psychometric Theory. New York: McGraw-Hill.

NYE, F. I. (1964) "Field research," in H. T. Christensen (ed.) Handbook of Marriage and the Family. Chicago: Rand-McNally.

OLSON, D. H. (1977) "Insider's and outsider's view of relationships: research studies," in G. Levinger and H. Rausch (eds.) Close Relations. Amherst: University of Massachusetts Press.

———(1981) "Family typologies: bridging family research and family therapy," in E. E. Filsinger and R. A. Lewis (eds.) Assessing Marriage: New Behavioral Approaches. Beverly Hills, CA: Sage.

———and C. RABUNSKY (1972) "Validity of four measures of family power." Journal of Marriage and the Family 34: 224-234.

OLSON, D. H. and R. G. RYDER (1970) "Inventory of marital conflicts (IMC): an experimental interaction procedure." Journal of Marriage and the Family 22: 443-448.

OLSON, D. H., H. I. McCUBBIN, H. BARNES, A. LARSEN, M. MUXEN, and M. WILSON (1982) Family Inventories. St. Paul: Department of Family Social Science, University of Minnesota.

OSGOOD, C. E., G. J. SUCI, and P. H. TANNENBAUM (1957) The Measurement of Meaning. Urbana: University of Illinois Press.

OTTO, L. B., V.R.A. CALL, and K. I. SPENCER (1981) Design for a Study of Entry into Careers. Lexington, MA: D. C. Heath.

PARSONS, T. and R. F. BALES (1955) Family, Socialization, and Interaction Process. Glencoe, IL: Free Press.

PINEO, P. C. (1961) "Disenchantment in the later years of marriage." Marriage and Family Living 23: 3-11.

POPPER, K. (1965) Conjectures and Refutations: The Growth of Scientific Knowledge. New York: Basic Books.

RAUSH, H. L., W. A. HERTEL, and M. A. SWAIN (1974) Communication, Conflict, and Marriage. San Francisco: Jossey-Bass.

REISS, D. (1981) The Family's Construction of Reality. Cambridge, MA: Harvard University Press.

REISS, I. L. (1967) The Social Context of Premarital Sexual Permissiveness. New York: Holt, Rinehart, & Winston.

———and B. C. MILLER (1979) "Heterosexual permissiveness: a theoretical analysis," pp. 57-100 in W. R. Burr et al. (eds.) Contemporary Theories About the Family (vol. 1). New York: Free Press.

REISS, I. L., R. E. ANDERSON, and G. C. SPONAUGLE (1980) "A multivariate model of the determinants of extramarital sexual permissiveness." Journal of Marriage and the Family 42: 395-411.

REYNOLDS, P. D. (1979) Ethical Dilemmas and Social Science Research. San Francisco: Jossey-Bass.

RISKIN, J. and E. E. FAUNCE (1970) "Family interaction scales, III: Discussion of methodology and substantive findings." Archives of General Psychiatry 22: 527-537.

———(1972) "An evaluative review of family interaction research." Family Process 11: 365-455.

ROBINSON, J. P. and P. R. SHAVER (1969) Measures of Social Psychological Attitudes. Ann Arbor: University of Michigan Press.

ROLLINS, B. C. and K. L. CANNON (1974) "Marital satisfaction over the family cycle: a reevaluation." Journal of Marriage and the Family 32: 20-27.

ROLLINS, B. C. and H. FELDMAN (1970) "Marital satisfaction over the family life cycle." Journal of Marriage and the Family 32: 20-27.

ROSENBLATT, P. C. (1974) "Behavior in public places: comparison of couples accompanied and unaccompanied by children." Journal of Marriage and the Family 4: 750-755.

RYDER, R. (1973) "Longitudinal data relating marital satisfaction and having a child." Journal of Marriage and the Family 35: 15-38.

SACKETT, G. P. (1978) "The lag sequential analysis of contingency and cyclicity in behavioral interaction research," in J. D. Osofsky (ed.) Handbook of Infant Development. New York: John Wiley.

SCHUMAN, H. (1982) "Artifacts are in the mind of the beholder." American Sociologist 17: 21-28.

———and S. PRESSER (1977) "Question working as an independent variable in survey analysis." Sociological Methods and Research 6: 151-170.

———(1979) "The open and closed question." American Sociological Review 44: 692-712.

———(1981) Questions and Answers in Attitude Surveys: Experiments on the Effects of Question Form, Wording, and Context. New York: Academic.

SCHUMM, W. R., H. L. BARNES, S. R. BOLLMAN, A. P. JURICH, and G. A. MILLIKEN (1985) "Approaches to the statistical analysis of family data." Home Economics Research Journal 14: 112-122.

SHUMM, W. R., W. T. SOUTHERLY, and C. R. FIGLEY (1980) "Stumbling block or stepping stone: path analysis in family studies." Journal of Marriage and the Family 42: 251-262.

SELLTIZ, C., L. S. WRIGHTSMAN, and S. W. COOK (1976) Research Methods in Social Relations (3rd ed.). New York: Holt, Rinehart & Winston.

SEWARD, R. R. (1978) The American Family: A Demographic History. Beverly Hills, CA: Sage.

SHARPLEY, C. F. and D. G. CROSS (1982) "A psychometric evaluation of the Spanier Dyadic Adjustment Scale." Journal of Marriage and the Family 44: 739-741.

SHAW, M. W. and J. M. WRIGHT (1967) Scales for the Measurement of Attitudes. San Francisco: McGraw-Hill.

SNIDER, J. G. and C. E. OSGOOD (1969) Semantic Differential Technique: A Sourcebook. Hawthorne, NY: Aldine.

Society for Research in Child Development (1973) Ethical Standards for Research with Children. Chicago: Author.

SÖRBOM, D. and D. G. JÖRESKOG (1981) "The use of LISREL in sociological model building," in D. J. Jackson and E. F. Borgatta (eds.) Factor Analysis and Measurement in Sociological Research. Beverly Hills, CA: Sage.

SPANIER, G. B. (1976) "Measuring dyadic adjustment: new scales for assessing the quality of marriage and similar dyads." Journal of Marriage and the Family 38: 15-28.

———and L. THOMPSON (1982) "A confirmatory analysis of the Dyadic Adjustment Scale." Journal of Marriage and the Family 44: 731-738.

SPANIER, G. B., R. A. LEWIS, and C. L. COLE (1975) "Marital adjustment over the family life cycle: the issue of curvilinearity." Journal of Marriage and the Family 37: 263-275.

STEINGLASS, P. (1980) "Assessing families in their own homes." American Journal of Psychiatry 127: 1523-1529.

STEVENS, S. S. (1951) "Mathematics, measurement, and psychophysics," in S. S. Stevens (ed.) Handbook of Experimental Psychology. New York: John Wiley.

STEWARD, D. W. (1984) Secondary Research: Information Sources and Methods. Beverly Hills, CA: Sage.

STRAUS, M. A. (1964) "Measuring families," in H. T. Christensen (ed.) Handbook of Marriage and the Family. Chicago: Rand-McNally.

———(1969) Family Measurement Techniques. Minneapolis: University of Minnesota Press.

———(1979) "Measuring conflict and violence: the conflict tactics (CT) scales." Journal of Marriage and the Family 40: 75-81.

———and B. W. BROWN (1978) Family Measurement Techniques: Abstracts of Published Measurements: 1935-1974 (rev. ed.). Minneapolis: University of Minnesota Press.

STRAUS, M. A. and I. TALLMAN (1971) "SIMFAM: a technique for observational measurement and experimental study of families," in J. Aldous et al. (eds.) Family Problem Solving. Hinsdale, IL: Dryden.

STRAUS, M. A., R. J. GELLES, and S. STEINMETZ (1980) Behind Closed Doors: Violence in the American Family. Garden City, NY: Anchor Press/Doubleday.

STRODTBECK, F. L. (1950) "Husband-wife interaction over revealed differences." American Sociological Review 16: 468-473.

———(1951) "The family as a three-person group." American Sociological Review 19: 23-29.

SUDMAN, S. (1976) Applied Sampling. New York: Academic.

TABACHNICK, B. G. and L. S. FIDELL (1983) Using Multivariate Statistics. New York: Harper & Row.

TALLMAN, I., L. R. WILSON, and M. A. STRAUS (1974) "SIMCAR: a game simulation method for cross-cultural family research." Social Science Information 13: 121-144.

TEACHMAN, J. D. (1983) "Early marriage, premarital fertility, and marital dissolution." Journal of Family Issues 4: 105-126.

THOMPSON, D. (1981) "The ethics of social experimentation: the case of the DIME." Public Policy 3: 369-398.

THOMSON, E. and R. WILLIAMS (1982) "Beyond wives' family sociology: A method for analyzing couple data." Journal of Marriage and the Family 44 (November): 999-1008.

THORNTON, A. and D. CAMBURN (1983) "The influence of the family on premarital sexual attitudes and behavior." Revision of a paper presented at the Annual Meetings of the American Sociological Association.

THORNTON, A., D. S. FREEDMAN, and D. CAMBURN (1982) "Obtaining respondent cooperation in family panel studies." Sociological Methods and Research 11: 33-51.

TIGGLE, R. B., M. D. PETERS, H. H. KELLEY, and J. VINCENT (1982) "Correlational and discrepancy indices of understanding and their relation to marital satisfaction." Journal of Marriage and the Family 44: 209-215.

U.S. Department of Health and Human Services (1983) "Children involved as subjects of research: additional protections." Federal Register 48, 46: March 8.

WAGENAAR, T. C. (1981) Readings for Social Research. Oxford, OH: Wadsworth.

WALKER, D. K. (1973) Socioemotional Measures for Preschool and Kindergarten Children. San Francisco: Jossey-Bass.

WALKER, K. and M. WOODS (1976) Time Use: A Measure of Household Production of Family Goods and Services. Washington, DC: Center for the Family, American Home Economics Association.

WAMPLER, K. S. and G. S. POWELL (1982) "The Barrett-Lennard Relationship Inventory as a measure of marital satisfaction." Family Relations 31: 139-145.

WEBB, E. J., D. T. CAMPBELL, R. D. SCHWARTZ, and L. SECHREST (1966) Unobtrusive Measures: Nonreactive Research in the Social Science. Chicago: Rand-McNally.

———and J. B. GROVE (1981) Non Reactive Measures in the Social Sciences. Boston: Houghton Mifflin.

WINTER, W. D. and A. J. FERREIRA [Eds.] (1969) Research in Family Interaction: Readings and Commentary. Palo Alto, CA: Science and Behavior Books.

WRIGLEY, E. A. and R. S. SCHOFIELD (1981) The Population History of England, 1541-1871. Cambridge, MA: Harvard University Press.

ZELLER, R. A. and E. G. CARMINES (1980) Measurement in Social Sciences: The Link Between Theory and Data. New York: Cambridge University Press.

ZELNIK, M., J. KANTNER, and K. FORD (1981) Sex and Pregnancy in Adolescence. Beverly Hills, CA: Sage.

Subject Index

Name Index

About the Author

Brent C. Miller is Professor of Family and Human Development at Utah State University. He received a B.S. in psychology from Weber State College (1971), an M.S. degree in Family and Human Development at Utah State University (1972), and a Ph.D. in Family Sociology at the University of Minnesota (1975). With David Olson he has coedited three volumes of a professional reference book entitled *Family Studies Review Yearbook* (1983, 1984, 1985) published by Sage. He also coauthored with Evelyn Duvall the sixth edition of *Marriage and Family Development* (Harper & Row, 1985). Dr. Miller has authored or coauthored over 40 peer-refereed articles, book chapters, and technical reports, as well as many popular articles. He is currently an associate editor for the *Journal of Marriage and the Family* and for *Family Relations*; he has been a guest reviewer for *Child Development, Family Process, Demography, Social Psychology Quarterly,* and several regional journals. Dr. Miller has consulted for the Office of Adolescent Pregnancy Programs (Department of Health and Human Services), the Social Science and Population Study Section of the National Institutes of Health, The Joseph P. Kennedy, Jr., Foundation, Community Health Clinics, Inc., and over a dozen national and international publishing houses. His general interests include marital qualities and normal developmental processes in marriage and family life, but his recent research has centered on adolescent sexual attitudes, behavior, and pregnancy, especially as these relate to family qualities and characteristics.